=======================================
STUDENT'S WORKBOOK
FOR
THE ART OF EDITING, 4/e
=======================================

STUDENT'S WORKBOOK

FOR

THE ART OF EDITING, 4/e

Brian S. Brooks

St. Louis Post-Dispatch
Distinguished Professor of Journalism
University of Missouri School of Journalism

Macmillan Publishing Company
New York
Collier Macmillan Publishers
London

Copyright © 1986 Brian S. Brooks

Printed in the United States of America

All rights reserved. No part of this book may be reproduced or transmitted in any form or by any means, electronic or mechanical, including photocopying, recording, or any information storage and retrieval system, without permission in writing from the Publisher.

Earlier editions, entitled *Contemporary Newspaper Editing: A Workbook for Students in Copy Editing,* copyright © 1976 and 1980 by Brian S. Brooks

Macmillan Publishing Co., Inc.
866 Third Avenue, New York, New York 10022

Collier Macmillan Canada, Inc.

Printing: 5 6 7 8   Year: 8 9 0 1 2 3

ISBN 0-02-315140-4

Preface

The third edition of *The Art of Editing* was the first to be accompanied by a workbook of exercises. The overwhelming success of that workbook is proof that many teachers nationwide shared my concerns about spending too many hours preparing exercises at the expense of more productive teaching activity. The availability of workbook exercises helps to solve that problem.

This updated version of the workbook gives teachers access to exercises that have been tried and tested by my students at the University of Missouri School of Journalism. Collectively, the exercises cover almost every point of editing that could be made in a copy-editing class.

I have prepared the exercises with both the teacher and student in mind. Instructions are specific when necessary but deliberately open-ended when, in my opinion, there is need for the teacher to guide the students closely. For example, teachers may choose to alter or supplement the instructions for layout exercises; no two teachers approach the subject alike.

The workbook is divided into six sections that correspond to the major blocks of instruction in the textbook. Each section opens with problems that can be used as out-of-class writing assignments or as in-class discussion topics. The exercises in the first four sections will help students translate textbook concepts into practical skills. The order in which the exercises appear reflects the manner in which most teachers approach the introductory copy-editing course. However, those who prefer to begin with headline writing or some other subject will find it easy to skip back and forth as they find necessary.

A few words about the appendixes are in order. Appendix I is a handy reference for those who cannot remember copy-editing symbols when they first begin editing. Appendix II is a headline schedule for those who choose to use it; some teachers may prefer to use their own. Appendixes III and IV are helpful in teaching students to check verifiable information: the spellings of names, the accuracy of addresses and similar items. Appendix V is a guide to layout, but again, some teachers may prefer a different approach.

This workbook is intended as a complement to the fourth edition of *The Art of Editing*. Despite that, either the workbook or the textbook can be used alone by teachers who prefer a different approach. I hope this workbook will help many teachers find the time to give more individual attention to students by relieving them of the burden of preparing exercises. It has done so for me. I also hope it helps students learn the fundamentals of copy editing by giving them an abundance of carefully constructed exercises on which to work. It has done so for my students, who deserve much of the credit for field-testing the exercises. I am forever indebted to them.

Brian S. Brooks
Columbia, Missouri

Contents

I. The Copy Editor in Perspective   1

    Problems   3

        The Copy Editor / The Copy Editor and the Reader / The Tools and How to Use Them

    Exercises   9

II. Copy-Editing Skills   19

    Problems   21

        The Editing Process / Protecting the Language / Style Notes / The Copy Editor on Guard / Legal Limitations on the Press / Handling the Wire

    Exercises   33

        Nouns and Pronouns / Verbs / Adjectives and Adverbs / Prepositions / Subject-Verb Agreement / Pronoun-Antecedent Agreement / Prepositions / Nouns and Pronouns / Subject-Verb Agreement / Pronoun-Antecedent Agreement / Adjectives and Adverbs / Verbs / Capitalization / Abbreviations and Acronyms / Punctuation and Hyphenation / Numerals / Grammar, Spelling, and Word Usage

III. Headline-Writing Skills   149

    Problems   151

        Creating the Headline / Avoiding Headline Problems

    Exercises   157

IV. Pictures, Graphics, and Design   207

    Problems   209

        Picture Editing / An Introduction to Type / Fundamentals of Newspaper Design / Contemporary Makeup and Design Practices / Makeup of Special Pages

    Exercises   219

V.	Editing for Other Media	259
	Problems	261
	Magazine Editing / Broadcast News Editing	
VI.	A Look to the Future	265
	Problems	267
	Newspapers and the Future	
I.	Symbols	271
	Copy Editing	273
	Proofreading	274
II.	Headline Schedule	275
III.	City Directory	279
IV.	Street Index	287
V.	Page Layout Aids	293
	Page Dimensions / Gutter-to-Gutter Column Widths / Other Calculations / Cutline Widths / Calculating Story Lengths	

SECTION I

THE COPY EDITOR IN PERSPECTIVE

Problems

THE COPY EDITOR

1. Describe in your own words the duties of a newspaper copy editor.

2. Talk with a copy editor for your local newspaper about his or her role at the newspaper. Focus specifically on job opportunities in copy editing. Using information obtained in the interview and from any other sources available, discuss job prospects in this field.

THE COPY EDITOR AND THE READER

1. Describe the major findings of Ruth Clark's latest research on newspaper readers. Describe how you, as an editor, would attempt to solve the problems posed by the results of her study.

2. Discuss the relationship of newspapers, television and other competing media. List the ways in which they complement each other as well as compete.

3. Briefly describe the Flesch formula, the fog index and the Dale-Chall formula. How do they differ, and what do they attempt to measure?

THE TOOLS AND HOW TO USE THEM

1. Describe the three major forms of copy-desk organization. Which form would you expect to find at a small daily of 8,000 circulation? Which form would you expect to find at a newspaper of 500,000 circulation?

2. List the titles of the five top-ranking editors of your local newspaper. Briefly describe the duties of each.

3. Outline in chart form the copy flow pattern used by your campus newspaper. In what ways would the copy flow pattern of the local city daily differ?

4. List the major copy processing systems in use at newspapers in the United States. Which one is used by your campus newspaper? Which one is used by your local city daily?

Exercises

Name _____ Course _____ Date _____

Edit the following sentences, using the proper copy-editing symbols (see Appendix I).

1. The Mayor sent the city manager to Keokuk, Iowa for the meeting.
2. Any top rated performer could draw a big crowd there.
3. She said six thousand people could not get into the arena.
4. Sergeant First Class Anna Lopez was in charge of the platoon.
5. Annettes brother was the Number One-ranked heavywieght contender.
6. He lives at 1926 West Boulevard South.
7. One of the biggest hits of all time was "Gone With the Wind."
8. Newspapers mail copies with special second class postage rates.
9. It was so hot the city used 123,000 gallons of water.
10. We are eager to help nations in need," the president said.
11. Workers toiled through the night to rescue those in the mine.
12. The Atlanta braves are challenging for the Western Division title.
13. "Tkae a hike!," he shouted in anger.
14. The best of the gymna sts was Mary Lou Retton.
15. The well known composer was born in Medford, Oregon, but moved to Los Angeles, CA, in 1983.
16. Peach trees are common in Georgia, and Magnolias often are associated with Mississippi.
17. Does the governore know What happened in the senate today?
18. He arrived in Rome at 7 p.m. Tues. night.
19. The sherriff said all deputies would start carrying 38-caliber revolvers.
20. The Orioles Baltimore are leading the Amercan League East.

—11—

Name _____ Course _____ Date _____

Edit the following sentences, using the proper copy-editing symbols (see Appendix I).

1. Taylor Electric Company is on Eighth Street.
2. New Yorkrs take such events in stride.
3. The last last time I saw you was in Columbia, S.c.
4. Military police arrested James E. Smithson, 19 of 201 E. Cherry St.
5. Troops exchanged fire today along the Sino Soviet border, Radio peking reported.
6. Graduation ceremonies have been scheuled for 3 pm Friday.
7. "I hope this is the end of it, he said.
8. Catholics and protestants exchanged gunfire in Belfast, No. Ireland.
9. Laguage skills are important to the journalist, the professor said.
10. "Then he said, 'Don't fire until you see the whites of their eyes."
11. Houston is one of the most humid cities in Tex.
12. It doesn't take long to drive from Washington D.C. to Baltimore.
13. "Luck has nothing do to with it," Marlow said.
14. The recieving deaprtment is in the rear of the store.
15. TV is a major source of entertainment for most americans, Rather said.
16. "Why didn't he hit it to right field?" the sportswriter asked.
17. Is America facing another guns-or-butter dilemma?
18. He starred on 'Father Knows Best' during the 1950's.
19. "The Electric Co." is a popular T.V. show for youngsters.
20. Col. Robert Lopez was 8th in his class at West Point.

Name _____ Course _____ Date _____

Correct the following stories using the proper proofreading symbols (see Appendix I).

The Police Department is offering a course entitled "Basic Firearms for Women," at 1 p.m. Sunday at the Police Building, 6th and Walnut streets.

Officer Wendell Mitchell said the the purpose of the program is to "familiarize women who might have handguns in the house." The program stresses gun safety, mitchell said, but the women also will practice shooting on the police pistol range.

The program has been offered several times during the last 2 years, Mitchell said. 'We've had really favorable responses to the class so far."

The class, which will be taught by Sgt. Steve M. "Steve" Stephens, is limited to 32 women, who will be acepted on a first-come, first-served basis. Mitchell said he expects the maximum number of participants.

Registration is this week from 8 am. to 4:30 p.m. through Thursday at the Police Bldg. A $2 registration fee covers the cost of materials, ammunitin, targets and .38-caliber service revolvers provided by police. Participants are welcome to bring their own handguns, Mitchell said, but he did not know if there would be time to practice with them. Those who choose to bring their own guns also must brng their own ammunition.

For further information contact the the plice Crime Prevention Unit at 874-7405.

Boone County Prosecuting Attorney Joe Moseley confirmed Monday that he offered prsecution immunity to a Harrisburg bank robbery suspect in exchange for information leading to the arrests of two other suspects in the robbery.

Walter Kidwell, 23, of Rt. 8, cooperated by identifying two alleged accomplices in the April 20 robbery of the Harrisburg branch of the American Bank of Centralia.

Kidwell was apprehended shortly after the robbery, but Boone County Sheriff Charlie Foster later that day said Kidwell was not a suspect.

However, with a guarantee of immunity, Kidwell confessed April 22 to an FBI agent and the next day an unientified 16-year-old Prathersville man was arrested in conneciton with the robbery.

Michael Dunham, 28, of Callaway County, was arrested Thursday by police in Morehead, Ken.

In addition to identifying the two suspects, Kidwell returned more than $3000, his share from his role in the robbery. Nearly $16,000 was taken in the robbery.

Kidwell still faces prosecution on charges of carying a concealed weapon when police found a set of brass knuckles in his possession at the time of his arrest. He was released April 22 on $10,000.

Name _____ Course _____ Date _____

Correct the following stories using the proper proofreading symbols (see Appendix I).

A restaurant in the southwest part of the city was robbed Monday night, making it the third robbery attempt on an eating establishment that day.

Police received a report of an armed robbery at Wendy's restaurant, 200 Business Loop W., at 11:30 p.m. Employees reported that the suspect entered the restarant through the rear door as an employe was returning from emptying the trash. The suspect displayed a handgun, demanded and collected money, and fled on foot with an undetermined amount of cash.

Early Monday, a man robbed the Interstate Pancake Howse, 1110 I-70 Drive, and a man with a similar description attempted to rob Burger King, 2015 W. Broadway within a 20-minute period.

The description of the Wendys suspect almost matched that of the other suspects, but police refused to say whether the crimes were committed by the same man.

Employees described the suspect as a black man, 20-30 years old, 6-foot 3-inches, 200 pounds, wearing a green full-length army type trench coat and a red ski cap.

The suspect who attempted to rob Burger King and the pancake house differed in height and in a few items of clthing. Employees described him as 5-foot 7-inches (1.6 meters) to 5-foot 10-inches (1.7 meters) tall. The man robbed the pancake house was wearing a red stocking mask underneath a blue, floppy hat, while the man who attempted to rob Burger King wore a red stocking cap.

The latest attempt was the 30th armed robbery in the city this year.

Residents must keep their weeds and grasses in control or face prosecution, according to the Department of health and Community Services.

Near average rainfall and above-normal temperatures this spring have contributed to the rapid growth of weeds and grasses here, said department Director Michael Sanford. The height of these plants must be kept at or below 12 inches, according to city ordinances.

If land owners need the help of a 3rd party to cut weeds or grass, they can contact the departent at 874-7345 for a listt of individuals who mow weeds and grass.

While the department will refer inquiries to these individuals, it does not guarantee their work.

LYONS, Kan. (AP) — Five members of an endangered species flew into the Quivira National Wildllife Refuge in central Kansas Wednesday, but they didn't stay long.

"We saw them early this morning, a little after 7," refuge manager Charles Darling said of the whooping cranes. "They were loafing around and feeding a little in the marsh."

The birds arrived at the refuge sometime during the night Tuesday and flew away by late morning on their journey from their winter home in the Aransas National Wildlife Refuge on the Texas Gulf Coast to Wood Buffalo National Park in Canada, Darling said.

SECTION II

COPY-EDITING SKILLS

Problems

THE EDITING PROCESS

1. Discuss the responsibilities of the copy editor. Can you add to the list in the textbook?

2. In your opinion, which of the characteristics of good writing is most important? Why?

3. Clip from your local newspaper a story in which the writer used the classic inverted pyramid approach. Could the writer have used a different approach? If so, rewrite the first five paragraphs, using the approach you would choose.

4. Discuss the role of the copy editor in relation to the role of the reporter. Pay particular attention to the role of the copy editor in altering or not altering the writer's style.

PROTECTING THE LANGUAGE

1. Search through your local newspaper for grammatical and spelling errors. List those you can find and correct the errors.

2. Check your local newspaper for circumlocutions. Show how you would correct the errors you find.

STYLE NOTES

1. Check your local newspaper for deviations from wire service style. Note whether the deviations seem to be intentional or in error.

2. Clip any six-inch story from your local newspaper. List all style points that apply to passages in the story.

THE COPY EDITOR ON GUARD

1. You are assigned to edit a story about the election of a 32-year-old as mayor. The reporter has written that he is the youngest mayor in the city's history, but you doubt the accuracy of that statement. Describe the steps you would take to check the information.

2. A reporter attributes a quotation to President John F. Kennedy. You believe the quotation came from the inaugural address of President Ronald Reagan. Describe the steps you would take to check the source of the quotation.

LEGAL LIMITATIONS ON THE PRESS

1. Your newspaper has learned that the mayor of your city had a homosexual affair with a fellow soldier during the Korean war. Discuss both the legal and ethical implications of printing the story.

2. If you later learned that the mayor's homosexual partner had been awarded three city contracts, would that affect the situation outlined in Question 1?

3. You are searching for an illustration for a story about mentally retarded children. You remember a photograph of a mentally retarded child that appeared in the newspaper two years ago. Would it be permissible to retrieve that photo from the morgue and publish it with the current story? Why or why not?

4. Discuss the differences in libel protection afforded to newspapers with respect to private individuals, public figures and public officials.

HANDLING THE WIRE

1. Your wire service transmits a new lead for a breaking news story, but you like the earlier lead better. Which would you use? If you choose the earlier lead, what further checks would be necessary to make sure that the story is still accurate?

2. Using newspapers available to you, find competing wire service accounts of an event. Make certain the publication date is the same. Compare the two accounts and tell which you would have selected if both had been available to your newspaper. Explain your decision.

3. Describe the services provided by the major wire services and tell how they differ.

4. Take two wire service accounts of the same incident and write a new story with information from both.

Exercises

Name	Course	Date

Identify the parts of speech in the following passages by indicating the usage above each word.

If the Treasury Department has its way, the government will waltz its way into the Alvin Ailey Dance Theater in an unwelcome way.

Donald Moss, manager of the non-profit company, said tax reform proposals being pushed by the Treasury Department and some members of Congress would affect the troupe drastically.

Moss, like others involved with charitable organizations, is concerned that tax proposals now before Congress will reduce incentives for people to donate.

Now list the verbs or verb phrases in the above passage and indicate the person, number, tense, voice and mood of each.

Verb or phrase	Person	Number	Tense	Voice	Mood

Name _____ Course _____ Date _____

Identify the parts of speech in the following passages by indicating the usage above each word.

    The simplest way to tell if an official is telling the truth is to check government documents, the executive director of Investigative Reporters and Editors said Monday at IRE's annual convention.

    Steve Weinberg, IRE executive director since 1984, said journalists too often fail to check things that can be verified easily. Documents are the journalist's best ally when government officials are trying to conceal the affairs of the people, Weinberg said.

    Earlier, a prize-winning investigative reporter had told the same group he had relied on such documents in producing his stories.

Now list the verbs or verb phrases in the above passage and indicate the person, number, tense, voice and mood of each.

Verb or phrase	Person	Number	Tense	Voice	Mood

—36—

NOUNS AND PRONOUNS

Mark out the incorrect form of the pronoun.

1. Joe, Paul and (me, I) are going to St. Louis next week.
2. I thought that you, (he, him) and (she, her) would work more.
3. The woman in the car was thought to be (I, me).
4. (She, Her) who wins the contest will receive the certificate.
5. The suspect said that it was not (she, her) who committed the crime.
6. The guilty persons, (she, her) and (he, him), confessed readily.
7. Did you enjoy (him, his) playing the guitar?
8. Give the report to (whoever, whomever) comes to the door.
9. Ask (whoever, whomever) you will, the answer is still the same.
10. I talked to the winners, (he, him) and (she, her).
11. It most certainly was not (he, him) or (I, me).
12. Award the certificate to (whoever, whomever) you believe to be deserving.
13. John Smith is 100; can you imagine (his, him) jogging?
14. The dean asked the chairman and (I, me) to come to his office.
15. He thought the young woman in the last row to be (I, me).
16. Don't you recall (him, his) asking us to do this?
17. No one recalls (who, whom) she said should work first.
18. (Who, Whom) did he say called him last night?
19. They have no objections to (you, your) going with them.
20. Both John Warren and (she, her) enjoyed the (instructor, instructor's) laughing at the remark.
21. Award the prize to (whoever, whomever) asks for it.
22. Award the prize to (whoever, whomever) she says should receive it.
23. The managing editor is making (we, us) writers a set of instructions.
24. (We, Us) early arrivals will have first choice of assignments.
25. Can you imagine (me, my) doing such a foolish thing?
26. Neither (he, him) nor his brothers are so short as (I, me).
27. The reporters were asked to meet (he, him) and (she, her) at the airport.
28. Was it (she, her) and (he, him)?
29. No one enjoyed (his, him) talking on that subject.
30. It is not (I, me) who am needed; it is (she, her).

Name _____ Course _____ Date _____

VERBS

Mark out the incorrect form within the parentheses.

1. The reporter spent her day off just (lying, laying) about the apartment.
2. He (lay, laid) the book on the desk.
3. She had (laid, lain) the report on the table.
4. John (lay, laid) down on the couch.
5. I saw your stylebook (lying, laying) on the desk.
6. The woman had just (lain, laid) down when the baby cried.
7. The doctor was (lying, laying) on the beach.
8. The writer (laid, lay) the story aside and answered the telephone.
9. The old dog likes to (lie, lay) in the shade.
10. The woman shouldn't have (laid, lain) in the sun so long.
11. The oil (lays, lies) near the surface.
12. The youngster's clothes were (lying, laying) about the house.
13. The nurse has been (sitting, setting) with the patient.
14. Police said the suspect just (set, sat) still.
15. The candidate decided to (set, sit) quietly and await the results of the vote.
16. Two children (setting, sitting) in the back seat of the car were not hurt.
17. The boy was told not to (sit, set) on the table.
18. The ushers (set, sat) extra chairs in the aisles.
19. The utility company (sat, set) the poles in concrete.
20. Fifty students (set, sat) waiting for the test to begin.
21. The children are (sitting, setting) in the trees.
22. The printers are (sitting, setting) type for the special section.
23. As a hospital volunteer, he often (sets, sits) up late with a patient.
24. If you (sit, set) on that chair, you may fall on the floor.
25. The Colorado River has been (rising, raising) all week.
26. The effect of the OPEC vote was to (rise, raise) oil prices again.
27. The players' hopes (raised, rose) and fell during the last quarter.
28. If gasoline prices (raise, rise) any higher, we shall have to sell the automobile.
29. The sun (raises, rises) at about 6 o'clock.
30. The cost of living is (raising, rising) rapidly.

31. The crew (raised, rose) the stage 3 feet.
32. The caller said he saw smoke (raising, rising) from the old building.
33. With its extra passenger, the helicopter would not (rise, raise).
34. According to market reports, stocks have been (raising, rising) rapidly.
35. The mayor expected his decision to quit as chairman of the committee and (accepted, excepted) his letter of resignation.
36. Did the reporter (lose, loose) all his keys?
37. Please (lend, loan) me your grammar book.
38. The noise from the construction project (aggravates, annoys, irritates) the students.
39. Some find that certain foods (aggravate, annoy, irritate) the skin.
40. The striking workers were told not to (aggravate, annoy, irritate) an already-tense situation.

Name _____ Course _____ Date _____

ADJECTIVES AND ADVERBS

Mark out the incorrect form within the parentheses.

1. Neither the mayor nor (he, him) (seem, seems) (happy, happily).
2. The landlord looked (angry, angrily) at Smith and (I, me).
3. The player looks (bad, badly) because of his injury.
4. Each woman (look, looks) (beautiful, beautifully) wearing (her, their) new outfit.
5. This drink tastes (sour, sourly) to (she, her) and (I, me).
6. From where we were working, the train's whistle sounded (loud, loudly).
7. The flowers (smell, smells) (sweet, sweetly) to (he, him).
8. The cook was told to cook the meat (tender, tenderly) so that it would taste (good, well).
9. The teacher in carpentry told (we, us) students to make a piece of furniture (strong, strongly).
10. (His, Him) taking another job (make, makes) (we, us) journalists feel (sad, sadly).
11. Boil the eggs (hard, hardly) while (she, her) sets the table.
12. Mary looked (happy, happily) because I believed (she, her).
13. The engine runs (smooth, smoothly) because (she, her) and (I, me) repaired it.
14. While Smith and (I, me) (was, were) camping, the thunder sounded (loud, loudly).
15. The editor looked (proud, proudly) as the panel honored both (she, her) and (he, him).
16. Each of the graduate students (is, are) (happy, happily) about passing (his, their) comprehensive examinations.
17. The soldier (seem, seems) (happy, happily) to return to the United States.
18. She (doesn't have but, has but) one television set.
19. (This, These) kind of apples is worth the price.
20. Bill is the (older, oldest) of the two students.
21. The teacher chose a (real, really) fine day for the trip.
22. The disc jockey has (a lot of, many) albums.
23. To publish a (more perfect, perfect) paper, we must work together.
24. Does he feel (sure, surely) that the reporter will keep his word?
25. (Sure, Surely) he feels that the reporter will keep his word.
26. The injured player feels (some, somewhat) better now.
27. The city editor (cannot help but laugh, cannot help laughing) when she recalls what the official said.
28. The news department (only has, has only) one video display terminal in operation.
29. See whether the reporter has (most, almost) completed the story.

30. The sportswriter said he has (quite a few, a number of) sources.
31. The copy editor edited the story (other, otherwise) than she was instructed.
32. Make the pizza crust (crisp, crisply).
33. The workers complained of feeling (poor, poorly).
34. The band played (poor, poorly) during halftime.
35. The children went to bed, but they (never, did not) (sleep, slept).
36. The new reporter is younger than (anyone, anyone else) on the staff.
37. The president looked (happy, happily) at his family as he took the oath of office.
38. The coach watched (proud, proudly) as his team received the trophy.
39. She (seldom ever, rarely) uses her bicycle.
40. The chief spoke (harsh, harshly) to the delinquent officers.
41. While camping, the group's supplies ran (low, lowly).
42. He is the most able of (any other, all) reporters on the newspaper staff.
43. The collector has stamps from (most, almost) all nations.
44. The managing editor seemed (rather, sort of) disgusted with the photography staff.
45. (Sure, Surely) the photographer was pleased to receive the honor.
46. The football players slept (sound, soundly) after the trip.
47. Prepare the steaks (rare, rarely) for Paula and (he, him).
48. Usually, the committee meetings are (real, really) dull.
49. The instructor looked (hopeful, hopefully) at the student.
50. A person should drive (careful, carefully).

PREPOSITIONS

Provide the correct preposition in each sentence. In some cases there may be more than one correct choice.

1. The sailors were told to go to _____ the ship.
2. The reporter was initiated _____ the professional society.
3. The kangaroo is peculiar _____ Australia.
4. The soldiers had to contend _____ the problem of low morale.
5. The newspaper's survey compared the features of foreign automobiles _____ the features of American automobiles.
6. The new police reporter was frightened _____ the idea of writing about organized crime.
7. Each player must adhere _____ the rules.
8. The finder of the lost billfold was rewarded _____ cash.
9. They can subscribe _____ more than one daily newspaper.
10. The reporter lives _____ Springfield _____ Providence Road.
11. The patient died _____ Legionnaire's disease.
12. The waiter was told to wait _____ three tables.
13. Mary Brown now lives _____ an apartment.
14. The car collided _____ the truck.
15. She wrote the story in accordance _____ the editor's instructions.
16. The editor spoke for 30 minutes _____ the new copyeditor.
17. Every student should listen attentively _____ the professor.
18. The streets run parallel _____ the city park.
19. The reporter was told not to meddle _____ matters of the city department.
20. Two committee members abstained _____ voting on the proposal.
21. Antonio Valdez prefers living on campus _____ living off campus.
22. Each reporter should concentrate _____ his or her work.
23. The story is almost free _____ style errors.
24. Friends confide _____ each other.
25. The writer was reluctant to part _____ the old typewriter.
26. Some people are not allergic _____ poison ivy.
27. Seniors dislike parting _____ classmates.
28. The reporter's work compares favorably _____ the work of another writer.
29. The managing editor told the reporter to try _____ complete the story before deadline.

30. The feature writer was disappointed _____ not getting the story.
31. The elderly man was accompanied _____ a hospital volunteer.
32. The officer's car was parked parallel _____ the other cars.
33. The news editor looked _____ while the repairman fixed the machine.
34. The commentator is careless _____ his appearance.
35. The news operation is independent _____ the advertising department.
36. According _____ the fire chief, the blaze could have been prevented.
37. In that sentence, the pronoun he is the antecedent _____ John Brown.
38. The car is parked _____ the house near the back door.
39. The train's passengers were deaf _____ the elderly woman's pleas for medical help.
40. The editor asked the reporter, "What do you infer _____ the mayor's comments?"
41. The copyeditor was told to substitute the second lead _____ the first lead.
42. The reporter is capable _____ writing the story.
43. The Police Department will keep the protesters _____ marching.
44. The jury did not agree _____ a verdict.
45. Mayor Smith said her aide is one _____ whom she can confide.
46. American automobiles vary _____ sizes.
47. The photographer was told to wait _____ the reporter _____ the newspaper's state bureau.
48. The striking truck drivers will issue a protest _____ the president's plan.
49. The president will speak _____ a joint session of Congress.
50. The professor arrived prior _____ the students.

Name _____ Course _____ Date _____

SUBJECT-VERB AGREEMENT

Mark out the incorrect form within the parentheses.

1. Smith, as well as Jones and (we, us), (was, were) late today.
2. Neither the chairman nor (she, her) (was, were) able to go to Washington.
3. (Has, Have) either Carter or (she, her) studied Latin?
4. Here (come, comes) the mayor and (they, them).
5. The editor and (I, me) thought it to be the coach and (she, her); however, neither (was, were) there.
6. (Was, Were) you and (she, her) in the restaurant when the reporter and (he, him) called?
7. Every one of the players (was, were) at the airport to meet Johnson and (I, me).
8. There (is, are) Hamilton and Fitzgerald, as well as (she, her), talking with the dean and (he, him).
9. (Has, Have) her sister and (he, him) decided to go with you, (she, her) and (they, them)?
10. The chairman, as well as the professors, (is, are) kind to Steve and (I, me).
11. Taylor, Jones and (I, me) (is, are) the committee.
12. A number of the members (has, have) visited Mary and (I, me).
13. Neither the chairman nor the professors (advise, advises) you and (I, me) to study Spanish next semester.
14. You, not (he, him), (is, are) the one (who, whom) the editor called.
15. Neither Joseph Watkins nor his son (was, were) able to assist (we, us) writers.
16. Susan, together with the rest of (we, us) juniors, (was, were) in Kansas, City, Mo., last weekend.
17. Every girl and boy (is, are) responsible to the teacher.
18. The jury (has, have) agreed upon a verdict.
19. The media (is, are) invited to the meeting.
20. Biscuits and gravy (is, are) on the menu.
21. Five percent of the workers (is, are) absent.
22. The number of persons present (is, are) large.
23. Five miles (is, are) a long distance to jog for someone (who, whom) you know to be unable to jog far.
24. The team (is, are) unable to reach a decision.
25. He is one of those persons (who, whom) (is, are) always late for class.
26. Many a one (has, have) been disappointed by another in (who, whom) he placed trust.
27. "Seven Beauties" (is, are) usually enjoyed by all (who, whom) understand Italian.
28. Magazines or books (is, are) an appropriate gift for (we, us) students.

29. Three fourths of the paper (has, have) been saved.
30. You and (she, her) (is, are) accountable to someone in authority.
31. Do you think $150 (is, are) too much for each of these speakers?
32. Here (come, comes) the reporters (who, whom) you wish to hire.
33. The team (is, are) going to Little Rock.
34. Steak and eggs (is, are) one of his favorite dishes.
35. This is one of those magazines that (is, are) popular with journalists (who, whom) you believe (is, are) well informed.
36. That she writes no better than (we, us) (is, are) an accepted truth.
37. Each graduate and undergraduate (is, are) insistent upon talking to an adviser (who, whom) the chairman believes can answer important questions.
38. That you were thought to be (he, him) (is, are) hard to prove.
39. Where (is, are) those students (who, whom) you called?
40. Today's news (is, are) important to the advertising department.
41. Not only (she, her) but also (he, him) (think, thinks) that you should be the winner.
42. The committee (has, have) gone to Milwaukee.
43. Ham and cheese (is, are) his favorite sandwich.
44. Neither the reporter nor the editors (has, have) studied metaphysics.
45. He, not his brothers, (is, are) attending classes at the University of Rhode Island.
46. Each of the 20 reporters (was, were) at the staff party.
47. Each member of the class (is, are) to receive a grade.
48. The woman (who, whom) you saw talking to the editor (was, were) (she, her) (who, whom) you have long respected.
49. Three students — you, (he, him) and (she, her) — were named.
50. The panel (is, are) Smith, Jones, Roberts, and Brown.

Name _____ Course _____ Date _____

PRONOUN-ANTECEDENT AGREEMENT

Mark out the incorrect form within the parentheses.

1. Every reporter and copyeditor (was, were) asked to give (his, their) aid to the special section.
2. Jacobs, as well as (we, us), (has, have) given (his, their) share.
3. Every one of you (is, are) responsible for (his, your, their) own copy.
4. Each writer must do (his, their) share.
5. No one wants to lose (his, their) books.
6. Not one of the clerks (has, have) had to decrease (his, their) work.
7. The students (has, have) lost (his, their) books.
8. Neither Taylor nor Ms. Blackman could find (his, her, their) books.
9. The police chief, as well as the officers, (was, were) willing to do (her, their) work.
10. No woman or man should praise (himself, themselves) too highly.
11. Everybody who seeks the job must send (his, their) résumé.
12. The panel (is, are) divided in (its, their) decision.
13. Not one of the reporters (think, thinks) that (he, him) can complete the story.
14. Every newspaper and magazine (has, have) (its, their) influence.
15. Each of the writers (has, have) put forth (his, their) best.
16. All persons should take care of (his, their) business.
17. Each person should take care of (his, their) business.
18. Either Brown or Smith will lend you (his, their) notes.
19. If anyone asks for me, tell (him, them) to call tomorrow.
20. Not one of the club members (is, are) doing (his, their) part.
21. No social worker cares to see (his, their) clients mistreated.
22. The man, as well as his brothers, (was, were) prepared to do (his, their) assignment.
23. Either Hancock or Ms. Reaves will offer you (his, her, their) advice.
24. Each of the scouts (has, have) completed (his, their) merit badge requirements.
25. The committee (is, are) not divided in (its, their) recommendation.

PREPOSITIONS

Provide the correct preposition in each sentence.

1. The reporter was initiated _____ the professional society.
2. The kangaroo is peculiar _____ Australia.
3. The soldiers had to contend _____ the problem of low morale.
4. The new police reporter was frightened _____ the idea of writing about organized crime.
5. The finder of the lost billfold was rewarded _____ cash.
6. The waiter was told to wait _____ three tables.
7. She wrote the story in accordance _____ the editor's instructions.
8. Two committee members abstained _____ voting on the proposal.
9. The managing editor told the reporter to try _____ complete the story before deadline.
10. The elderly man was accompanied _____ a hospital volunteer.

NOUNS AND PRONOUNS

Mark out the incorrect form within the parentheses.

1. Joe, Paul and (me, I) are going to Detroit next week.
2. I thought that you, (he, him) and (she, her) would work more.
3. The woman in the car was thought to be (I, me).
4. (She, Her) who wins the contest will receive the certificate.
5. Did you enjoy (him, his) playing the guitar?
6. Give the report to (whoever, whomever) comes to the door.
7. No one recalls (who, whom) she said should work first.
8. They have no objections to (you, your) going with them.
9. Yes, it was (they, them) about (who, whom) I was speaking.
10. It was (we, us) staff writers (who, whom) you saw.

SUBJECT-VERB AGREEMENT

Mark out the incorrect form within the parentheses.

1. Smith, as well as Jones and (we, us), (was, were) late today.

—49—

2. Neither the chairman nor (she, her) (was, were) able to go to Washington.
3. (Has, Have) either Carter or (she, her) studied Latin?
4. Here (come, comes) the mayor and (they, them).
5. There (is, are) Hamilton and Fitzgerald, as well as (she, her), talking with the dean and (he, him).
6. (Has, Have) her sister and (he, him) decided to go with you, (she, her) and (they, them)?
7. Taylor, Jones, and (I, me) (is, are) the committee.
8. Neither the chairman nor the professors (advise, advises) you and (I, me) to study Spanish next semester.
9. Susan, together with the rest of (we, us) juniors, (was, were) in Kansas City, Mo., last weekend.
10. The media (is, are) invited to the meeting.

PRONOUN-ANTECEDENT AGREEMENT

Mark out the incorrect form within the parentheses.

1. Every reporter and copy editor (was, were) asked to give (his, their) aid to the special section.
2. Jacobs, as well as (we, us), (has, have) given (his, their) share.
3. Every one of you (is, are) responsible for (his, your, their) own copy.
4. Each writer must do (his, their) share.
5. No one wants to lose (his, their) books.
6. Not one of the reporters (think, thinks) that (he, him) can complete the story.
7. Every newspaper and magazine (has, have) (its, their) influence.
8. If anyone asks for me, tell (him, them) to call tomorrow.
9. Each of the scouts (has, have) completed (his, their) merit badge requirements.
10. The committee (is, are) not divided in (its, their) recommendation.

ADJECTIVES AND ADVERBS

Mark out the incorrect form within the parentheses.

1. Neither the mayor nor (he, him) (seem, seems) (happy, happily).
2. The landlord looked (angry, angrily) at Smith and (I, me).
3. The player looks (bad, badly) because of his injury.
4. This drink tastes (sour, sourly) to (she, her) and (I, me).
5. The cook was told to cook the meat (tender, tenderly) so that it would taste (good, well).
6. The soldier (seem, seems) (happy, happily) to return to the United States.
7. She (doesn't have but, has but) one television set.
8. (This, These) kind of apples is worth the price.
9. Bill is the (older, oldest) of the two students.
10. (Sure, Surely) he feels that the reporter will keep his word.

VERBS

Mark out the incorrect form within the parentheses.

1. The reporter spent her day off just (laying, lying) about the apartment.
2. He (lay, laid) his book on the desk.
3. The woman had just (lain, laid) down when the baby cried.
4. The old dog likes to (lie, lay) in the shade.
5. The nurse has been (sitting, setting) with the patient.
6. The ushers (set, sat) extra chairs in the aisles.
7. The utility company (sat, set) the poles in concrete.
8. The Colorado River has been (rising, raising) all week.
9. The effect of the OPEC vote was to (rise, raise) oil prices again.
10. The players' hopes (raised, rose) and fell during the last quarter.

Circle the verbs in the passive voice in the following stories.

JOHANNESBURG, South Africa (UPI) -- Police and army troops sealed off a riot-torn black township Sunday to restore order and rout "terrorist" elements *blamed* for the murders of black moderates, officials said.

Adriaan Vlok, deputy minister of defense and law and order, said the operation *had been launched* after "numerous requests by law-abiding citizens of Kwanobuhle that effective steps *be taken* to normalize living conditions."

Kwanobuhle, about 20 miles northwest of Port Elizabeth and about 600 miles south of Johannesburg, has been a center of widespread racial violence that has claimed at least 150 lives this year.

VATICAN CITY (UPI) -- Pope John Paul II requested prayers Sunday for the success of his upcoming trip to Belgium, Luxembourg and the Netherlands, where threats against his life have spawned tight security precautions.

The pontiff, target of an unsuccessful assassination attempt in May 1981, made the request to 30,000 pilgrims and tourists *gathered* in St. Peter's Square for his regular Sunday blessing.

During his appearance, the Polish-born pope made no mention of the threats against his life in Holland and Belgium.

BRESCIA, Italy (UPI) -- President Sandro Pertini said Sunday he was happy to *have been honored* by the Soviet Union during the weekend "even if I am not a communist."

The Presidium of the Supreme Soviet announced Saturday it had awarded Pertini the "Order of the Patriotic War of the First Degree" in connection with the 40th anniversary of the end of World War II.

Pertini, a partisan during World War II who fought against Fascist dictator Benito Mussolini, said he *was pleased* with the award.

CANNES, France (UPI) -- A bomb explosion destroyed a Communist Party office near Cannes in southern France Sunday and shattered windows in nearby buildings, police said.

The explosive device *had been fashioned* out of a butane gas container and *planted* in front of the building, which *had been protected* only by an iron grill, police said. No one *was injured* in the 3 a.m. blast.

No claims *were made* immediately for the incident.

—53—

Name _____ Course _____ Date _____

ABBREVIATIONS AND ACRONYMS

Correct the style errors in the following sentences.

1. K.O.P.N. is a listener-supported fm radio station.
2. Miss Adams is one of six students in a diving class taught by Tom Rainey, manager of Diver's Village, 131 S. 7th Street.
3. The measure was introduced by Senator Edward Kennedy, D.-Massachusetts.
4. The DC10 crash in Chicago was a major disaster.
5. Some believe that the quality of products made in the U.S. is slipping.
6. The F.B.I. said it would cooperate fully with the CIA.
7. He lives at Ninth and Elm streets.
8. Soldiers stayed on guard at Ft. Knox, and the gold supply remained secure.
9. The U.S. voted against the U.N. resolution condemning Israeli occupation of the land.
10. Roy Fenton, Jr., of 114 Maple Avenue, said he will call Atty. Gen. Ralph Oliver the next time he has a complaint.
11. Oklahoma finished No. 1 in the Big Eight for the third year in a row.
12. He said the American Hospital Assn. would decide the issue next month.
13. Earl C. Bryden, 54, of 734 Demaret Dr., was the defendant
14. He watched a documentary about the B1 bomber on TV.
15. She rode AMTRAK for the 1st time in 1977.

CAPITALIZATION

Correct the style errors in the following sentences.

1. He sat in the dressing room gulping the remains of a Waldorf salad, a few French fries, and a nerve-soothing Manhattan cocktail.
2. Schneider has a Psychology degree he received last year from the university of Kansas.
3. The Pope sent the president a message.
4. The New York Yankees signed Outfielder Dave Winfield to a multi-year contract.
5. According to Werner erhard, "the truth believed is a lie."
6. Kellerman left the east after college, traveling west to realize his dreams in Hollywood.
7. The Associated Press stylebook is a journalist's Bible.
8. Sen. William Proxmire Awarded his Golden Fleece trophy to the energy department for giving $1,200 to Doug Elley of Lupus, Mo., for his "Skyscrapper," a solar-powered outhouse.
9. Ralph, Mrs. Smith's Bassett Hound, disappeared Sunday.
10. Former president Jimmy Carter said he is content to work on his memoirs.
11. The president said constitutional guarantees are sufficient and no legislation by Congress would help.
12. The Boston city council will meet at 7 P.M. Monday.
13. The crime is a federal offense.
14. Men from earth may visit Mars before the turn of the century.
15. The Rocky mountains are the highest in the United States.

Name _____ Course _____ Date _____

PUNCTUATION AND HYPHENATION
Correct the style errors in the following sentences.

1. He is the president of Smith Foods Co., Inc.
2. "Who's going to change the light bulb?," she asked.
3. Stephen Crane wrote "The Red Badge of Courage".
4. He was given a five- to 10-year prison sentence.
5. He is a first class fiddle player who is known throughout the area she said.
6. The minister said he was certain that the incident had parallels to Jesus's life.
7. He conducted a postmortem on the postdoctoral student.
8. The exconvicts' group meets once-a-month at the Presbyterian Church.
9. Elvis Presley was known to millions as the King of Rock 'n' Roll.
10. Teachers salaries should be competitive with those of other districts'.
11. "For appearance's sake," he said, "We decided it would be better to hire an auditing firm.
12. The music he produces is played mostly on Mexican American stations.
13. "Music and art are important parts of education, he said. "Without them it would be a drab world."
14. Miller Danielson, 29, of Hays, Kan. was indicted.
15. "He said, "Throw it down", so I did."

Name _____   Course _____   Date _____

NUMERALS

Correct the style errors in the following sentences.

1. The Sixth U.S. Circuit Court of Appeals ruled that the case did not involve the 1st Amendment.
2. The $6,800,000 fund would be used to help farmers hurt by the drought.
3. The St. Louis Cardinals beat the Green Bay Packers 24 to 14.
4. He said the odds were 5–1 that the Dodgers would not repeat as champions.
5. Sunday's high will be about 29 degrees Fahrenheit.
6. Irving Malestrom, twenty-one, and Jill Solomon, 19, will be married on Jan. 19th.
7. He lives at 3, 008 Paris Rd., which is in the 3rd Ward.
8. Housing costs are expected to soar more than ten per cent annually during the '80s.
9. 74 more students are expected to enroll this year.
10. 1981 was a very good year for the rock group.
11. The sermon should start about 10:00 a.m., he said.
12. His amendment would cut funding for the measure by ¼.
13. He had received 3459 responses to the questionnaire by Sunday.
14. He is the number one student in a class of 153.
15. She said the value of a share of IBM Stock fell 1¼ points in less than 2 hours.

GRAMMAR, SPELLING, AND WORD USAGE
Correct the style errors in the following sentences.

1. Bailey said it was difficult deciding between the three candidates for gov.
2. The team (that was comprised of two men and seven women) won it's first game 9—2.
3. He said the fire began when someone lay some plastic parts too near the furnace. Before anyone noticed, he said, the blaze was well underway.
4. Farley said he didn't know who among the teen-agers present at the time was involved in the theft.
5. "We don't have enough aides to accommodate all the patients," Reinhardt said.
6. Hopefully, the U.S. won't have to actually call up the men who registered for the draft, he said.
7. Welles said the city was looking for someone that is familiar with the kinds of problems Columbia faces and whom has several years experience as a City Manager
8. "This Fall," Hendrick said, "the state should face up to the problem of toxic wastes and pass stringent legislation against dumping them."
9. The committee's concensus was that less people would probably attend the festival this year as a result of the violence that marred it last year.
10. When the camper stopped, Simmons woke up and stepped out of the back to see what was wrong. But his wife Mary didn't know that, and drove off without him.

Name _____ Course _____ Date _____

Correct the style errors in the following sentences.

1. The first meeting of the committee will be at 2 p.m., Sun., Jan. 26.
2. Sergeant First Class Bill Simpson has been assigned to an army outpost in Alaska.
3. Rev. James Jones will lead the congregation in singing.
4. County Bank is at Eighth and Broadway.
5. The Secretary of Defense said yesterday in Minneapolis the President will not make a decision before Feb. 1.
6. Dallas, Texas, is one of the leading cities in the southwest.
7. Abbreviations of more than two letters usually do not require periods, but there are exceptions, including U.S.S.R.
8. He lives at 809 Springer Terr.
9. A buss is a vehicle and a bus is a kiss.
10. Communist Party leaders said they hope to make Communism a way of life in the country.

Name _____ Course _____ Date _____
_____

Correct the style errors in the following sentences.

1. She lives at 15 Main Street.
2. Defense Attorney John Jacobs said yesterday he will appeal the decision of the supreme court.
3. The former President of the U.S. announced his support of John Jones, Jr. for United States senator.
4. Miami, Florida is one of the largest cities in the south.
5. There were more than sixty persons waiting in line.
6. She waited at the airport in N.Y. for over 6 hours.
7. "Its very cold to day, she said.
8. Sec. of State Rogelio Solis said he expects a record turnout for the election.
9. Smith & Co., Inc. is moving from 16 East 16th Street to Four Maple Road.
10. The city counsel will meet at 3 p.m., Fr., November 7.

Name _____ Course _____ Date _____

Correct the style errors in the following sentences.

1. The 16-kilometer (10-mile) race was won by Igor Stanovich of the Soviet Union.
2. The Saint Louis Blues hockey club is expected to play an exhibition game at the Hearnes Multipurpose Building.
3. The family was happy that the kidnappers kept their word.
4. John R. Simpson, 32, 2703 Meadowlark Lane was arrested Sept. 1 and charged with drunk driving.
5. The 17-year-old girl was 5 foot 2.
6. I-70 is the primary East-West highway in the state.
7. Former Sen. Walter Mondale was his party's presidential candidate in 1984.
8. The low bid was submitted by Simmons Construction Company in the amount of $2,345 dollars.
9. Ft. Smith, Ark. is near the Okla. border and is no longer an army base.
10. The newly-chosen officers will take office October 1 in ceremonies in Washington D.C.
11. Sergeant First Class Ron Oakland has been assigned to Fort Sill, Okla., where he will be a Drill Instructor.
12. The Federal Bureau of Investigation issued a nationwide bulletin for Ralph Larkin, Tulsa, Oklahoma, in connection with the murder in which a 38-caliber pistol was used.

Name _____ Course _____ Date _____

_____

Correct the style errors in the following sentences.

1. Richard Gray, former city manager, said Ray Beck, Public Works Director, was one of his best employes.
2. The House ways and means committee will meet at 3 p.m. Friday to discuss the president's proposals.
3. Dr. John Kuhlman, professor of economics at the University, will teach the course this semester.
4. The Rev. Mr. Monk Bryan served at First United Methodist Church before becoming a bishop.
5. First National Bank has lowered its prime interest rate to 13 per cent.
6. The Republican party chose Kansas City, Missouri for the site of it's convention.
7. An Ozark Airlines DC9 limped into Lambert Field in St. Louis after brushing a light aircraft above Belleville, Illinois.
8. Bob Pugh, ex-mayor, lives at 502 West Rock Creek Dr.
9. Many believe the U.S. should not contribute so muct to N.A.T.O.
10. The 6th U.S. Circuit Court of appeals was expected to issue its decision in February, 1985.
11. Former U.S. Rep. Jerry Litton (D.-Mo.) was killed in a plane crash after winning the senatorial nomination.
12. The board of directors will meet Fri.
13. Sen. Sam Rausch, Fr., D-New Hampshire, asked if the company had attempted to influence the dicision with a contribution of $3,800,000.
14. The Senate vote on the ammendment by Representative Smith was 235 to 189.
15. The freshmen class is large, but not the largest in history.

Name _____ Course _____ Date _____

_____

Correct the style errors in the following sentences.

1. The senate voted 54–38 Monday to cut the Agriculture Department budget by 10%.
2. The United States Constitution provides that no president may seize control of the military.
3. He was born in Boise, Idaho December 19, 1927 to the late John and Mary Simpson.
4. The last vote on the issue was in May 1981 when it was defeated by ten votes.
5. Mayor Rodney Smith, First Ward Councilman Pat Barnes and Fifth Ward Councilman Barbara McDonald voted against it.
6. The Communist Party and the Socialist Workers party have been unable to win spots on the state ballot.
7. The president said he will spend 2 days at Camp David, Md. preparing for his address to congress.
8. Ft. Benning, Ga. is the home of the infantry.
9. Over 3,000 students went to the polls, the campus newspaper reported.
10. Congress is trying to decide whether to provide funds for the B-1 bomber, the intended replacement for aging B-52's.
11. Teen-agers are to meet with the city council at 7 p.m. Monday.
12. The U.N. was the scene of the worst confrontation of U.S. and Soviet diplomats in sixteen years.
13. Lawmen searched the five-country area, but were unable to find clues to the murder.
14. A 22 caliber pistol was used in the shooting, said Ted Boehm, Sheriff.
15. Rep. Wilbur Mills (D-Ark.) was chairman of the Ways and Means Committee until the Tidal Basin incident in 1975.
16. High mass will be said at the church Sunday at 9 a.m., said the Most Rev. John Kelly, bishop of the diocese.
17. His investments were values at 11 million dollars, but he couldn't afford 10¢ for a cup of coffee.
18. The man who robbed the store was 5 foot 8 with blonde hair and blue eyes, Police Chief William Dye said.
19. The president expects much help from 16 and 17-year-old campaign workers in his bid for reelection.
20. James Michener's book, "Hawaii," was a best seller for many months.

Name _____ Course _____ Date _____

Edit the following sentences to eliminate verbosity.

1. The ushers collected the sum of $5.40.
2. The meeting, which was held last night, began at 7:30 p.m. in the Municipal Building.
3. The company is engaged in the construction of several motels.
4. In the event that it rains, the game will be postponed.
5. Police believe he was strangled to death.
6. It reverts back to the former subject.
7. She was met by a screaming throng of persons.
8. The man fell a distance of 50 feet.
9. A bolt of lightning struck the house.
10. A great number of times he's wrong.
11. The petition did not get a sufficient number of signatures.
12. The building was a flaming inferno.
13. A good fireman learns to descend down the pole rapidly.
14. The car was moving with a rapid amount of speed.
15. In excess of 300 persons attended the show.
16. At the present time he is available.
17. Everyone, with the exception of John, was included.
18. That city often gets snow during the winter months.
19. At the conclusion of the meeting it was obvious there was no agreement.
20. He was absolutely certain he could still sing.

Name _____ Course _____ Date _____

Edit the following sentences to eliminate verbosity.

1. The store is located at the corner of Ninth and Elm Streets.
2. A new graduate course in communications law is being introduced this semester for the first time.
3. The firm of Johnson & O'Hare, Inc. entered a bid of $3,571.
4. Those who are majoring in environmental physiology are few in number.
5. All of a sudden the supply was exhausted.
6. The show begins at 7 p.m. Sunday night in the auditorium.
7. Floodwaters entirely destroyed the town despite the fact that there was a floodwall surrounding it.
8. For a period of 10 days, workmen labored in excess of 12 hours daily to complete the new building.
9. James McGregor is going to inform those in the immediate vicinity of the leak to evacuate.
10. In view of the fact that the restaurant is no longer accepting advance reservations, we cannot eat there.
11. That bald-headed man is the father of a baby boy born Saturday.
12. Steve Miller said he was kicked off of the team.
13. The appellate court remanded the case back to Boone County Circuit Court.
14. Nixon tendered his resignation after being confronted with the evidence.
15. Underground subways are common in New York and some European cities.
16. Police said he was a self-confessed killer.
17. The odor of onion still persists because neither of the two of you has taken out the garbage.
18. The CIA is an agency charged with foreign, not domestic, intelligence responsibilities.
19. The chairman received his education at Tulane University in New Orleans.
20. He was the husband of Anna Schaeffer, who died in the early 1970s, about 1972.

Name _____ Course _____ Date _____

Edit the following sentences to eliminate verbosity.

1. The train was moving with a rapid amount of speed.
2. The swimmer set a new speed record.
3. The car was totally destroyed.
4. The late John Jones' widow was caught in a downpour of rain.
5. A bolt of lightning hit the house and totally destroyed the roof.
6. There is not a sufficient amount of paper for every student in the class.
7. The Jewish rabbi is the father of the baby girl born Saturday.
8. A great number of times it rains here.
9. In the event that the plane is late, the meeting will be postponed until later.
10. Police believe that the old man was strangled to death.
11. At the present time she is waiting for the commencement of her class to begin.
12. All the children, with the exception of Billy, were invited to the birthday party.
13. The committee is meeting at 7 p.m. Sunday night.
14. The attorney tendered his resignation after being found guilty of public drunkenness.
15. A fence completely surrounded the farm.
16. At the conclusion of his speech, the senator called on persons in the audience to express their true opinions.
17. The suitcase weighed in excess of 50 pounds.
18. The factory was a flaming inferno and was completely destroyed by morning.
19. At the conclusion of the summer months, most children are ready to return back to school.
20. The group descended down the mountain quickly.

Name _____ **Course** _____ **Date** _____

Edit this story as directed by your instructor.

Firemen

    The Personnel Advisory board will meet at 7:30 p.m. tonight to hear a grievance filed by Local 1055 of the International Association of Fire Fighters.

    The local is contesting the denial of a merit raise to firefighter Gene Windmiller. Local 1055 Secretary Mel Tipton says the local contends Windmiller was unfairly and unscrupulously denied a raise because he used one of his fringe benefits, sick leave.

    The hearing tonight will be closed to the general public at the request of the local. The board will meet at 7 p.m. in the city council chamber of the County-City Bldg.

—30—

Name _____ Course _____ Date _____

Edit this story as directed by your instructor.

A free support group is being formed to provide counseling services to area families affected by the current farm fiscal-policy crisis.

Dan Birmingham and Mark Altomari of Associates in Human Services say they are donating their time in an effort to help families deal with the major financial hardships they face.

"We don't pretend to have all the answers to this problem," Birmingham says, "but we think there are some folks out there who are experiencing a tremendous amount of stress right now."

The group will meet at Office Plaza I, 2100 I-70 Drive S.W., on a weeknight to be determined by its members. Call 445-1016.

Name _____ Course _____ Date _____

Edit this story as directed by your instructor.

ACCIDENT

A man from Springfield fall from a scaffold Tuesday morning and hit a crossbeam and landed at the bottom of an empty water basin at the city water treatment plant in McBaine.

Dave Clark, 34, was sandblasting the wall off a one-million-gallon watter softening basin when he fell from the ten-foot sacffold.

"He hit his head on a beam above him and lost his balance, said Ralph whitehead of St. Louis. Whitehead is construction manager for Busch and Latta, a Painting company working at the water treatment plant.

Clark was taken to the County Hospital after he was lifted on a stretcher from the 18 foot tank by the fire dept. rescue squad. Clark was reported in good condition.

—30—

Name _____ Course _____ Date _____

Edit this story as directed by your instructor.

FRAUD

Police have recieved several reports recently of telephone credit card fraud, according to a news release from Capt. Caroll W. Highbarger.

Highbarger describes this type of fraud as follows: Callers claim to represent a company sponsoring a contest in which credit card numbers were chosen randomly to select winners of a valuable prize. Those receiving the calls are asked to recite their credit card numbers to verify that the company is calling the correct person. If the credit card number is given, it can be used to make charges that defraud businesses and cause problems for the credit card holder.

People who believe they may have been the victim of such a crime should call the Police Department at 874-7428.

Name _____ Course _____ Date _____

Edit this story as directed by your instructor.

BOARD

The Board of Adjustment last night approved building a 45-60 foot tower for cable television.

Pat Scott, City Clerk, said the special meeting was held in order that the International TelemeterCorporation could start work on the tower by June 10 to provide cable television service on schedule. The next regularly scheduled board meeting was on June 21.

The tower at 4116 Clark Lane will receive waves beamed from N.Y. and Atlanta via a communication satellite.

David Rogers, the corporation's lawyer, said the tower will not involve high voltage, will not interfere with local raido and television stations and can withstand winds up to 125 miles per hour. The corporation has received a permit from the Federal Communications Commission to build the tower.

In other business, the Board gave its approval to a request from the Southwest Swim Club, College Park at Oxford St., to build a 96-square-foot addition to its club house.

Name _____ Course _____ Date _____

Edit this story as directed by your instructor.

GARAGE

Construction of the downtown parking garage scheduled to begin in May could temporarily worsen the parking shortage it is intended to alleviate.

In an effort to avoid parking probelms caused by the loss of 98 spaces north of the County-City Building, City Manager Richard Grey suggested Thrusday that the city lease property outside of downtown and provide a "free" shuttle service for city employees, business people and shop owners and their employees to downtown.

If city employees and business people who now use the lot start parking on the street, they will use spaces needed by downtown shoppers, Gray said.

During a noon luncheon of city and county officials Thursday, Gray said the city was negotiating for open land that could be used as a parking lot and leased on a short-term basis.

A shuttle bus would run from 7:30 a.m. to 8:30 p.m. and from 4:30 p.m. to 4:30 p.m. Monday through Friday.

For people doing business at the County-City Building, 24-minute meters will be installed on the north, west and south sides of the building. One aspect of the plan Gray believes might be unpopular is the enforcement of parking meter regulations for all parked cars.

Name _____ Course _____ Date _____

Edit this story as directed by your instructor.

YEARGIN-OBIT

Marge N. Yeargin, 87, of Rural Route 7, passed away Saturday at the County Hospital.

Mrs. Yeargin, was born February 12, 1902 in Newark, Ohio to Joseph O. and Essie Lou Reed Johnson. She married Ross O. Yaergin on Jan. 27, 1929 in Knasas City. He preceded her in death.

Ms. Yeargin was active in the County League of Woman Voters for the last fifteen years. She also was member of the Oakland Christian Church.

Survivors include three sons: Jesse B. yeargin, of Denver, Colorado; Russell B. Yeargin of 3435 East Willow St., and Howard R. Yeargin, Route 9, Two daughters Mrs. Willie Mayo, Route 9, and Mary Yeargin, of the home, and two grandchildren. A sister and brother preceded her in death also.

Services for Mrs. Yeargin will be at 2:00 p.m. Thursday afternoon at the Oakland Christian Church, with Rev. Alfred Orr officiating. Burial will be completed at Oakland Cemetary.

Friends may call at Parkers Chapel any time Thursday prior to the service.

—30—

Name _____ Course _____ Date _____

Edit this story as directed by your instructor.

UNITED

The United Way today awarded $27,312 in supplemental appropriations to three agencies whose programs were threatened by inadequate funding.

The United Way Board of Directors gave $15,137 to the Rape Crisis Center to enable the center to operate through the end of the current physical year. Director Karen Gunter said the supplemental funds will help pay her salary and those of two part-time professional counsellors.

The United Way board also awarded $10,000 to the Front Door, a personal crisis counseling center which caters to those with drug abuse and alcohol probelems. The agency will use the funds to pay higher rent at its new facility, 211 Hitt St. The old facility was condemned by the city.

A supplemental appropriation of $3,175 will go to the Boy Scouts for a sumeer camp program for disadvantaged youths. The amount matches a similar sum given to the Girl Scouts during the regular funding process.

Earlier the board had appropriated $1.37 million for 68 agencies in the county.

—30—

Name _____ Course _____ Date _____

Edit this story as directed by your instructor.

ARREST

Two victims of a robbery led city law enforcement authorities to the arrest of one suspect a short time after the incident occurred Monday night.

Arrested was James L. Lawhorn, 18, 301 5th Street. He was charged with stealing and is being held in the county jail in lieu of bond totaling $2,000.

Police reported that Rosie James, age 23 and Glenda Estep age 23 both of 1005 N. Eighth Street, were making out deposit slips outside the Commerce Bank, 500 Bus. Loop 60 West when two men approached them.

When Ms. Extep attempted to drop an envelope containing a sum of $30 into the night depository, one of the two males grabbed the envelope, shoved her aside and ran.

The other man then grabbed the envelope Ms. james was filling out, which also contained $30 and followed his companion, police said.

The two women told police they followed in their car until the men split up and ran through some backyards. They saw 1 man minutes later and called the police for lhep.

—30—

Edit this story as directed by your instructor.

MURDER

Five days of hearings ended Friday before a Michigan judge, with a statement from a witness who said former Fayette resident Charles Fisher, charged with the murder of his wife, thought she was having an extramarital affair.

Fisher, 45, a former Central Methodist College biology professor, is charged with the first-degree murder of Ella Maria Mercado "Ria" Fisher, 32. She was found July 15 with her head wrapped with tape in their Ann Arbor, Mich., home.

Mrs. Fisher's father, Manuel Mercado, told the court Fisher believed his wife was planning to go to Germany on July 17 where her cousin, Javier Hurtado, 30, was studying. Fisher accused Hurtado of being a communist or socialist, Mercado said.

According to Police Officer William Keppen who investigated the murder case, Mercado testified that Fisher "pleaded with him to intercede and stop the air trip."

The hearings concluded in 35th District Court at Plymouth, Mich., and Fisher was bound over for trial in the Wayne County Court in Detroit, Mich. He is free after posting 10 percent of his $250,000 bond.

more

Murder - add one

At the hearings, Fisher told the court he came home from his job as a microbiologist at the veteran's hospital in Ann Arbor in mid-afternoon July 14, and was in bed asleep before his wife, who was employed by the Medical Personnel Pool in Detroit, came home from her shift.

A neighbor of the couple, however, testified that she saw Fisher driving in a red pickup truck with two other men at 8:30p.m. on the night of the murder. Her statement conflicts with testimony given by Fisher, who said he did not leave after he came home from work at 3:30p.m.

Fisher said an intruder with "a soft, soothing voice," woke him and demanded his money and keys to his pickup truck. The intruder fled and Fisher said he discovered his wife bound and gagged with adhesive duct tape.

Fisher has claimed the truck was stolen by the intruder; the pickup was later found about 30 miles from the Fishers' residence.

Edit this story as directed by your instructor.

COURT

Today's meeting of the Boone County Court represents the beginning of the end of next year's budget preparations. The county's budget officer, Presiding Judge Billie Tritscher, will present a tentative budget to the other court members.

As the court inspects Tritschler's proposals, other county officers will be listening to figure out how much their salary requests have been axed. Requests for increases have ranged from six per cent to 15 per cent, but most county officeholders fear that their requested increases will be cut.

Tritschler said on Monday that those fears are justified. "Salaries are going to be a very, very great disappointment to people" who work for the county, she said.

The only substantial increase in county revenue from this year, Tritschler said, will be from revenue sharing. The exact amount coming from the Federal government will be determined at a revenue-sharing hearing later this month.

All county officeholders this fall have come before the court to justify requests for their departments. But in the long run, Tritschler does most of the trimming of the budget.

more

Court - add one

Between now and the final budget approval date, February 30, the court will be busy. The preliminary revenue-sharing hearing scheduled for January 19, will give county officers and the general public an opportunity to suggest uses for Federal money.

-30-

Name _____ Course _____ Date _____

Edit this story as directed by your instructor.

MALPRAC

    A local doctor Monday filed a motion to dismiss the medical malpractice suit filed against him.

    L.W. Lucas of 1 E. Broadway said in the motion filed in county circuit clerk's office that the counts "fail to state a claim...upon which relief can be granted."

    The suit, charging malpractive and wrongful death, was filed Jan 28 with circuit clerk's office. Also named in the suit are James D. Nanson of 401 Keene and Hugh S. Harris Ju. of 801 Cowan Drive, two local doctors; and Janet Dillavou of 5580 Teton Drive, a licensed practical nurse.

    Each defendant was charged with a single malpractice count and they all were charged with the one mass count.

    Richard Collins of Morgan County is bringing suit on behalf of James and Heather Collins, the children of Brends Collins.

    The suit says Lucas, Nanson, Harris and Dillavou caused or increased the risk of death for Brenda Collins. It goes on to say that Collins' death March 8, 1983, was

                        more

Malprac - add one

the result of a "pulmonary air embolism created by (the) disconnection of tubes inserted into her body for the purpose of providing life-sustaining support and treatment..."

An embolism is the blockage of a blood vessel created by a blood clot, air bubble, clumps of bacteria, small drops of fat, cancer cells or other foreign objects.

Erwin Milne, an attorney representing Richard Collins, Heather Collins and James Collins, said Brenda Collins was recuperating from a gallbladder operation.

The count against Dillavou also says Collins was left "totally unattended in her hospital room for several minutes shortly after surgery and as a direct result crawled or fell out of bed to the floor and lay upon the floor unattended for several munutes before the unsuccessful efforts to resuscitate her even began.

-30-

Name _____ **Course** _____ **Date** _____

Edit this story as directed by your instructor.

Storm

    A howling thunderstorm accompanied by 54-mile per hour winds viciously slashed thru the area late yesterday afternoon, causing power failures in about 100 homes.

    Telephone service was disrupted in another 100 homes and transmissions of a local television station were interrupted.

    Robert Alderson, general manager of Boone Electric Cooperative said major power failures were the result when a line in Hartsburg and a line north of town at Highway 63 and County Route NN were blown down.

    Alderson said other widely dispersed cessations of power were caused by downed trees and transformers struck by lightening. Alderson said three crews completed repairs by 8 p.m. last night.

    "With the high winds that went through here, we were lucky it didn't do more damage than it did, Alderson said.

    The maurauding storm was more violent and ruthless south of town, uprooting trees and tearing away limbs.

    Richard Koenig, general manager of KCBJ-tv (Channel 19) said the station was knocked right off the air because of damage to the Tipton-based utility company that serves the station.

                          more

Storm — add one

    Telephone company spokesmen said there was so extensive damage to any of its equipment, despite the temporary telephone service failure.

—30—

Edit this story as directed by your instructor.

TEACH

School officials are planning a career ladder that would reward teachers for quality performance.

Assistant Superintendent of Schools James Ritter said thecareer ladder would be developed by a committee of teachers, administrators and Board of Education members. The committee could have proposals ready for the board in three to four months for a possible pilot program this fall.

A career ladder would give pay hikes to teachers who score well on an evaluation based on performance, education and peer evaluation.

"We have actually looked at it for some tine," Ritter said, "but we may not be able to do it for a year."

The board has not polled teachers about career ladder, Ritter said.

Mary Sadich, president of the Community Teachers Association, said the committee that studied merit pay last year will begin looking at career ladders soon.

The idea comes at a time when many taechers want better salaries. Average pay for area teachers is $20,980, some $2,557 below national averages.

more

Teach - add one

"Once base pay is up then we can consider a career ladder," Sadich said. "I think that is our primary objective, but maybe we need a career ladder for incentive."

Teachers who get career ladder benefits would also have additional responsibilities, including summer work or helping new teachers, Ritter said. Involvement in any career ladder would be voluntary, while participation in merit pay would be mandatory.

Merit pay, which is opposed by many teachers, is based on a teacher's education and experience. Unlike career ladders, merit pay raises are decide only be administrators, not teachers The bonus goes only to a certain percent of teachers and comes from money earmarked for all teacher's salaries.

-30-

Name _____ Course _____ Date _____

Edit this story as directed by your instructor.

Suit

By Maurice Gosfield
Staff Writer

The wife of a Fayette man crushed to death by a hydraulic loading machine in Jan. '84 has filed a $380,000 suit against the foreign corporation that manufactured the machine, claiming the company is resposible for her late husband's death.

Mary E. Ricik filed the civil suit against the K.K. Kase Co. in Boone County Circuit Court yesterday. In the suit the Mrs. Ricik charges that the company-built fork-lift and its component parts were defectively designed and manufactured, causin g the death of Rupert Ricik on Jan. 16, 1978.

Ricik, 47, was found crushed between one of the machine's arms and the engine housing at the Community Rehabilitation Center warehouse, 1101 Hinxson Avenue, where he was an employee. There weren't any witnesses to the accident, but Ricik was last seen unloading a trailer full of paper with the fork-lift.

Policemen said that Ricik apparently was leaning over the side of the loader when he either struck a lever controlling the machine's forklift or the engine shut off, causing the arms of the

more

Suit — add one

lift to fall. Ricik was pronounced dead at the scene when a Boone Co. ambulance arrived.

In the lawsuit, Mrs. Ricik claims she was deprived of care, protection, support and maintenance of her husband and sole support for herself and partial support for two minor children. She is asking for personal damages of $38,000.

-30-

Name _____ Course _____ Date _____

Edit this story as directed by your instructor.

CHOCOLATE

Chocoholic dieters can now share the "miracle" of Canfield's Diet Chocolate Fudge Soda, which has been compared to a hot fudge sundae by a Chicago columnist.

Bob Greene, whose column appears in 80 newspapers across the country, satrted a nationwide carze for the soda, which is normally distributed only in Illinois, Indiana, Michigan, Wisconsin and Iowa. In his Jan. 23 column, Greene called the diet pop a two-calorie miracle which had enabled him to keep off the 22 lbs. he lost two years ago.

In the three weeks after Greene's column appeared, the Chicago-based Canfield's Beverage Co. sold over 2 million cans of Diet Chocolate Fudge Soda, twice the amount sold in all of the previous year.

By the end of those three weeks, local supermarkets began to try to get the soda into the area.

Although the local grocers haven't experienced the frantic demand for the soda that made Page 1 headlines ("The Hunt Is On," and Ohio newspaper proclained), reactions has been good, says Stuart Elmore, grocery manager at the North County store.

more

Chocolate - add one

"The first two people I saw as I was building the display were two young gals who came by and said, 'Canfields'...all right!' They were just ecstatic about it," says Elmore. The store sold over 100 cases the first weekend.

Canfield's Diet Chocolate Fudge Soda is made up entirely of artificial ingredients. What Canfield's did was to combine the proper combination of chemicals to precisely duplicate the taste of chocolate fudge, keeping in mind the taste of a Hershey bar.

That uniqueness had Canfield's producing 1,200 cans of soda a minute in a 24-hour production of the Diet Chocolate Fudge Soda. Still they were not able to keep up with the demand, which Alan Canfield, senior vice president, has compared to th craze for Cabbage Patch Dolls.

Ironically, the man who started the Canfield's craze, Bob Greene, has now had a problem. Because of the incredible demand caused by his column, he said in a column last month, he couldn't find any Canfield's Diet Chocolate Fudge Soda.

-30-

Edit this story as directed by your instructor.

HOSPITAL

The Boone Hospital Center Board of Trusties today okayed the Hospital's $17.4-million operating budget for next year, which includes a semiprivate room rate increase of about nine percent and an overall salary increase for employes of about seven per cent.

The new budget, which represents a 13 per cent increase over this year's budget, will take effect January 1st.

Semiprivate room rates at the Hospital will go from $97 to $104 a day. Private room rates will be hiked at a slightly lower rate, from $108 to $112 per day.

Even with the rate increase, the Hospital's operating report predicts that the average adult daily census for next year will be 224.66 patients. The Hospital has 316 beds, and Hospital spokesperson Patsy Brill said that the average daily occupancy rate "will stay about the same as this year or increase only slightly." The Hospital had an occupancy rate of 74.9% last year.

The overall salary increase is an attempt by hospital administrators to stay competetive in the job market for qualified personnel while keeping in line with average national salarly increases of seven per cent, Brill said. Hospital

more

Hospital - add one

employes will get varying amounts of increases by pay classification, the average of which will be seven per cent, Brill explained.

The whole budget, Brill said, represents an attempt by the hospital to hold down hospital expenditures in keepings with the objectives established by the Voluntary Cost Effectiveness Program -- a cooperative statewide effort of hospitals, physicians, health insurance companies, hospital suppliers and consumers -- to hold the line on health care expenditures.

VCEP's objective is to work towards an annual reduction of two per cent in the rate of increase in hospital expenditures. Boone Hospital's budget is a reduction of somewhere around four per cent in that rate of increase. "There is no fat in this budget," Brill said.

"Although we realize that hospital costs will continue to rise," he said, "we are committed to keeping our increase as low as possible." He noted that hospitals are a labor-intense industry and have no control over inflationary pressures in purchasing food, petroleum-based products and energy.

In other action, Brill told the Board that about 25 open-heart operations have been performed at the Hospital since the program started last month, and that about 150 open-heart operations are expected to be performed next year. He said the hospital should have no trouble meeting Department of HEW guidelines, which recommend that a hospital perform 75 open-heart operations in the first year of such a program.

-30-

Edit this story as directed by your instructor.

BOARD

By T. Wayne Kendall
Staff writer

The Board of Education will meet Monday to review the results of a recent survey to determine the need for a separate "traditional" school.

The meeting is set for 7:30 p.m. Monday night at the board's office, 1818 W. Worley.

A traditional school characterized by strict discipline, self contained classrooms and an emphasis on basic skills, could provide residents with an alternative public school in a seperate facility.

Preliminary results of the survey, sent to more than 3,500 parents of children in kindergarten through grade 5, indicated that only two to three per cent of those responding desired such a school. But 25 to 30 per cent said they favored more traditional approaches to education within the existing schools, in at least some areas.

The preliminary evaluation was based on about 1,400 survey questionaires which were returned by the last board meeting.

more

BOARD — add one

About 450 more questionaires have been received since then.

The board also will recieve recommendations from Charles Campbell, representative of the Marshall & Brown architectural firm, to determine steps to be taken in the acoustical treatment of the music facility at Hickman High School.

Although previous measures to improve acoustics in the music room have been taken by the Board, such sound-absorbing materials as acoustical tiles still may be needed.

At the Monday night meeting, Jay Willows, Director of Vocational Education, will discuss plans naming the new area vocational school facility under construction at Rock Bridge High School. The Board will hear special reports from various school officials as well.

In other business the Board will:

*Take action on the proposed revisions in Board of Education policies;

*Approve the recently established per-pupil cost for non-resident tuition;

*Hear a report on proposals for developing additional athletic facilities at Rock Bridge High School;

*Hear a report on a proposed insurance policy which extends school insurance coverage.

—30—

Edit this story as directed by your instructor.

Plunge

Two men were killed late last night when their tractor-trailer rig plunged off the Missouri River bridge 12 miles west of the city.

James L. Jiminez, 27, and Robert L. Radford, 34, both of Shawnee Mission, Kans., were pronounced dead at the scene, about 10 miles west of the city, by Boone County Medical Examiner Richard Threlkeld after their rig went out of control in the westbound lane of Interstate 70 and plunged 75 feet to the riverbank below.

Boone County Sheriff Charlie Foster said both probably were killed instantly, either from the impact of smashing through the guard railing on the bridge or when the vehicle smashed to the ground below.

Foster said the men were returning to their suburban Kansas City homes after a trip to Indianapolis when the wreck occured. They had delivered a truck load of flour for the Pillsbury Co., for whom they work. Foster said Jiminex was single but Radford was divorced. His wife and two children now live in Reno, Nev., where his wife words as a bar maid.

Rogers L. Leviticus, 45, of Alhambra, Ala. was following the

more

plunge--first add

truck when the accident occurred. "He just lost control of it," Levitus said. "It looked like he went to sleep at the wheel and just plunged into the hands of the Lord."

Leviticus, a Baptist faith-healer on his way to a revival in Manhattan, Kans., said there was a spectacular noise as the huge rig crashed onto the riverbank. "If they had been 30 yards ahead of where they were, they would have plunged into the river channel and the police would still be fishing for their bodies." he said. "The Lord works in starnge ways sometimes."

Foster said it was impossible to tell if Radford, who apparently, was driving, actually fell asleep as Leviticus surmised or if a mechanical problem caused the wreck.

Boone County Fire Protection District engines were dispatched to the scene, but there was no fire or oxplosion. "We always go to wrecks like this to make sure the vehicles don't burst into flames," said Chief Steve Paulsell. "Diesel fuel is less volatile, than gasoline, though, so there was no problem." Paulsell's extrication crew had to cut the men's bodies from the mangled wreckage of the rig in an operation that took almost 1½ hours.

The bodies of the men were transferred to Boone County Hospital and subsequently taken to Memorial Funeral Home. Elkins Funeral Home of Shawnee Mission is handling funeral services for the two.

The accident took place about 10:30 p.m. Monday.

—30—

Name _____ Course _____ Date _____

Edit this story as directed by your instructor.

HOUSES

Two houses owned by County Hospital have been vacant and deteriorating for more than a year, a candidate for the hospital Board of Trustees said Thursday.

Walter Johnson, a board candidate in the April 2 election, said the houses are the public's property, and he doesn't understand why the hospital let the properties decay.

According the Johnson, Jack Blaylock of Cannon and Blaylock Realtors values the houses at 407 and 411 S. Ann St. at about $86,000.

Johnson said he is distressed to find that a major resource in idle and depreciating: "Every month that sale is delayed the (hospital) loses interest, and the property value declines.

"It's the public's property over there," Johnson said, "and I don't like what happened."

Referring to the condition of the property, Johnson said, "I doubt that anyone would call that responsible management, and it is not responsible to the neighbors."

more

Houses - add one

The houses were placed on the market in December but have not been sold, probably because of their poor condition, neighbors said.

Neighbors are upset about the properties' condition. Some did not know the hospital owned the houses.

"It disturbs me that the hospital is not interested in the quality of the neighborhood," said Stephen Buckles of 1623 University Ave., whose house borders the two for sale.

"It sure looks like the houses have been broken into and that someone has been living in one. There is food and clothing in one of the houses, and the toilet has been used, too."

"Windows have been broken and the lawn have not been kept up on a regular basis. In fact, the hospital let the pipes freeze last winter, and a toilet stool sits in the front yard of one of the homes," Buckles said.

A prospective buyer of the properties, Steve Ladlie, said he looked at the houses two weeks ago.

"I can't believe the hospital let them run down that bad," Ladlie said. "The appraisal of the property is extremely high. One of the houses has an extremely bad structural flaw in the foundation."

Board Chairman Jack Estes referred questions to the hospital administration.

more

Houses - add two

"I am not aware of the day-to-day condition of the houses," Estes said. "Randy Morrow (a hospital assistant vice president) could better hadnle questions about particular facts concerning the property since he's taking offers for the purchase of the two houses."

Morrow refused to comment Thursday night. "Call me at my office," he said.

Because the properties are woned by a government agency, no taxes are paid on them. Johnson said returning the properties to the tax rolls would benefit local government.

"And I'm sure the hospital can use the interest on $86,000."

Name _____ Course _____ Date _____
_____

Edit this story as directed by your instructor.

PEGGY

    Since 1941, Peggy Rhynsburger has been a part of the Camp Fire tradition here.

    Peggy Rhynsburger, also know to members of the organization as "Miss Peggy," was involved in the Camp Fire Council from 1941 to 1953, a period of growth and change for the organization. Her early work became the foundation for today's program, and many of the girls in her program have carried on her traditions.

    This year, the organization celebrates the 75th year anniversary of its founding in Maine. Locally, a birthday celebration will be held from 2p.m. to 5p.m. March 24 at the Cosmopolitan Recreation Center.

    The theme of the 75th birthday party is "Celebrate 75 Years of Camp Fire Friendships." Past, present, and future members and volunteers of Camp Fire, Inc. will be honored. There will be singing, a ceremony, refreshments and a finale of helium balloons set free to symbolize the growth of Camp Fire.

                              more

Peggy - add one

The contributions of Rhynsburger and other past volunteers of Camp Fire will be noted at the celebration. Their work helped make great strides in the development of Camp Fire youth organization.

Locally, the organization has clubs from the first to ninth grades. Camp Fire Girls was chartered in the 1920's for young girls; boys could join after 1975 and in 1979 the word "Girls" was dropped from the name.

The organization was intended to be an educational, non-denominational group for girls. Rhynsburger brought together the formerly segregated black and white clubs.

"The most satisfactory thing that happened when I was director was that we became an integrated camp six years before the Supreme Court decision to integrate schoold," Rhynsburger said.

"I believe in the brotherhood of man, with the help of white parents and black parents we did a great deal."

She ran a resident camp in the summer called Camp Tee Pee Toto, and the with of parents and board members at the opening of each season, it was a success. The fathers of the campers formed a group called the "Do-Dads," who built a dining hall, tents, and the wooden floors in each.

"It was very primitive," Rhynsburger said "Once they made a shower - the water came from a creek and it was 30-40 degrees - bery cold."

more

Peggy - add two

She acquired the name "Miss Peggy" because the children couldn't say Rhynsburger. Shelly Brandenburg, a current bolunteer Camp Fire leader, still refers to her as "Miss Peggy."

Rhynsburger described one of her favorite duties as a camp director, getting the children up at 7 in the morning.

"We had a P.A. system in the dining hall and we played music for them. For the Blue Birds, grades 1-3, it was "lazy Mary Will You Get Up" and for the older girls we played "Oh What A Beautiful Morning."

The present council camp, Camp Takiminia, received similar treatment in the 1960s.

Rhynsburger is presently recovering from knee surgery, but says she hopes to attend the birthday celebration on March 24.

Lee Ann Mazurka, current executive director of the Bonne Femme Council, said a few goals camp Fire wants to accomplish are to make children more independent, self-reliant and to help them develop self esteem. We also want to to teach them things they wouldn't learn at home," Mazurka said.

One of the projects local clubs are working on this year is raising money for the restoration of the Statue of Liberty. It is call the Save Our Statue project and and each club earns the right to participate by learning something about the history and restoration of the statue.

more

Peggy - add three

"Camp Fire is diong good things here. It is growing and we want people to know about it," Mazurka said.

-30-

Name _____ Course _____ Date _____

Edit this wire copy as directed by your instructor.

BOMB

    CANNES, France (UPI) -- A bomb explosion destroyed a Communist Party office near Cannes in southern France Tuesday and shattered windows in nearby buildings, police said.

    The explosive device was fashioned out of a butane gas container and planted in front of the building, which was protected only by an iron grill, police said. No one was injured in the 3 a.m. blast.

    No claims were made immediately for the incident.

    upi 06-05 12:12 ped

Name _____ Course _____ Date _____

Edit this wire copy as directed by your instructor.

PRESS

ROME (UPI) -- Italian journalists, who have staged chronic strikes recently to press their demands for big pay increases, signed a new three-year contract Tuesday that promises salary hikes totaling $190 a week.

Leaders of the journalists federation, FNSI, reached agreement with management early Tuesday after 19 hours of uninterrupted bargaining led by Labor Undersecretary Andrea Borruso, officials said.

The agreement provides for raises totaling $190 over the next three years. Journalists will receive $50 a week more backdated from January 1985, another $40 beginning in July, and additional $50 pay raises in April 1986 and in March 1987.

    upi 09-24 12:19 ped

Name _____ Course _____ Date _____

Edit this wire copy as directed by your instructor.

SUDAN

KHARTOUM, Sudan (UPI) -- Palestine Liberation Organization Chairman Yasser Arafat arrived today for two days of talks with the Sudanese leadership.

In an arrival statement, Arafat said he was visiting Sudan "to share the joys of victory with the Sudanese people who participated with us in our battles."

The visit was the first by the PLO chairman to Sudan since the military overthrew President Jaafar Numeiry and seized power.

"Proceeding from the deep-rooted ties between the Sudanese and Palestinian peoples, I felt it a must upon me to come here and participate with the revolution command and the great Sudanese people in their joys," Arafat said.

upi 04-02 12:37 ped

Name _____ Course _____ Date _____

Edit this wire copy as directed by your instructor.

TAIWAN

    TAIPEI, Taiwan (UPI) -- Taiwanese and U.S. trade officials plan formal talks May 9 in Washington on a bilateral free trade agreement to remove import restrictions and reduce customs tariffs, the United Daily News reported Sunday.

    Informal discussions on such an agreement have been going on in Washington between Vincent C. Siew, director-general of Taiwan's Board of Foreign Trade, and Doral Cooper, assistant negotiator of the U.S. trade representative office, since Cooper first proposed the talks last week, the paper said.

    Topics expected to be negotiated at the May 9 talks include removal of both customs and non-tariff barriers to free trade, the paper said.

    Removal of non-tariff barriers might pose difficulties for Taiwan since it would entail throwing open the local market, the paper said.

    upi 05-05 02:03 ped

Edit this wire copy as directed by your instructor.

MISSION

LIMA, Peru (AP) -- Gunmen killed an American Baptist missionary over the weekend at his home in a Lima suburb, police said Sunday.

They said they were still trying to determine a motive for the Saturday shooting of Thomas Brown, 36, who was born in Illinois, but who spent the last nine years living and working in Lima as a pastor of the Baptist Bible Church.

Local newspapers quoted Brown's widow, Frances, as saying her husband was shot through the heart by four men armed with revolvers who seemed familiar with the family's home in the middle-class Puente Piedra district, 13 miles north of Lima.

Reports Sunday in Lima newspapers El Comercio and La Republica said Brown was killing during a robbery attempt. The Expreso newspaper said he was shot while trying to prevent the men from kidnapping his 17-year old daughter Maria. The newspapers said Brown had three children.

U.S. Embassy officials did not return repeated telephone calls from The Associated Press asking for information.

ap 05-06 12:43 pcs

Name _____ Course _____ Date _____

Edit this wire story as directed by your instructor.

CHARLES

VENICE, Italy (AP) -- The Prince and Princess of Wales passed the last afternoon of their 17-day sightseeing tour of Italy with a leisurely gondola cruise Sunday on the canals of Venice.

Charles and Diana waved to the crowds lining the canals as their gondola, steered by a specially chosen gondolier also know locally as "the Prince," passed by.

Earlier, Prince Charles, dressed in a double-breasted gray suit and Diana, in a green and blue suit with a huge, spectacular matching hat, watched the start of Venice's "Vogalonga" boat race.

The couple joined thousands of spectators in sending off the hundreds of boats, including canoes, traditional gondolas and the Venetian eight-ore festive "bissone" on the 20-mile non-competitive "race" in the Venice lagoon.

The already tight security surrounding the royal couple was beefed up following a Saturday night phone call to an Italian news agency in which the anonymous caller threatened that Sunday "will not be calm like the rest of their trip."

Police, however, did not give much credence to the message, which said that Sunday was the fourth anniversary of the death of imprisoned Irish Republican Army member Bobby Sands, who fasted to death.

ap 05-06 01:43 pcd

Name _____ Course _____ Date _____

Edit this wire story as directed by your instructor.

RIOTS

JOHANNESBURG, South Africa (AP) - Police and soldiers sealed off and occupied a black township in the eastern Cape Province Sunday to quell unrest as three more blacks were killed in overnight rioting, authorities said Sunday.

Also in the eastern Cape, bloody clashes erupted between rival black anti-apartheid groups. At least three blacks, including two children aged 3 and 5, have died in the in-fighting since Friday, news reports said.

Police headquarters in Pretoria said two men were shot dead by police and a third was found stabbed to death in continued unrest that the white-minority government says has left more than 200 dead since last September. Private groups say more than 300 have died.

In Kwanobuhle near Uitenhage in the eastern Cape, police shot dead a 27-year-old black man after arsonists set alight three houses belonging to policemen, a spokesman said in Pretoria. The body of a 48-year-old black man who was "killed with sharp instruments" was found in the same township.

Deputy Minister of Defense and Law and Order Adriaan Vlok said police and army units moved into Kwanobuhle at dawn "to restore order" early Sunday.

RIOTS--first add

    A Kwanobuhle resident who asked not to be named said several hundred soldiers stood a short distance apart on the main streets of the township, and police distributed pamphlets to residents calligri on them to help orestore order.
ap 08-03 8:48 aed

Name _____ Course _____ Date _____

Edit this wire story as directed by your instructor.

USED

WASHINGTON (AP) -- Whether they're called cream puffs of clunkers, second hand or previously owned, used cars sometimes break down. So, before buying one, consumers should think about who will pay for any repairs.

That's the message the Federal Trade Commission hopes to drive home with new regulations that will cover the nation's used-car dealers starting Thursday.

But, even before the rules can be shifted into gear, con sumer advocates are complaining that changes made last year eliminated most of the regulatory horsepower.

The main provision of the rule requires window stickers on used cars, telling buyers whether a car is being sold "as is", or if a warranty is offered; and giving other advice about such purchases.

"The most important piece of information that a used-car buyer can obtain is to find out from the dealer who is going to pay for repairs if something goes wrong after the sale. And that is exactly what this rule is going to do," said Carol Crawford, director of the Federal Trade Commission's Bureau of Consumer Protection.

MORE

USED--first add

The most prevalent problem found in a study of the used car market, she said, "was that cars were sold 'as is,' that is, without warranty, were being represented by the dealer as coming with a warranty."

But while the rule gives consumers a clear indication of whether they get warranty protection, a controversial provision that would have forced dealers to tell their customers about any defects they were aware of, was dropped from the regulation.

And it's that missing provision that has drawn the ire of consumer advocates.

"I think that the rule will go into effect without notice and without effect. It simply misses what consumers want to know when buying a car, and that is, what's wrong with it," said Clarence Ditlow, head of the Washington-based Center for Auto Safety.

"If they (the FTC) were serious about protecting consumers from unsafe autos, they would have required disclosure of known defects, rather than leaving it up to the buyer to make that determination," added Jack Gillis, author of "The Car Book," a buyers' guide to auto safety.

In fact, the scrapping of that provision drew a sharp rebuke from FTC Commissioner Patricia P. Bailey, who dissented in the 3-1 vote last fall when the new regulation was passed by the agency.

MORE

USED--second add

"The FTC's rulemaking authority is a potentially powerful tool for promoting consumer welfare, but this rule, without the known defects provision, is little more than a consumer education campaign masquerading as significant, industrywide regulation," said Ms. Bailey in her dissent.

And Rep. James J. Florio, D-N.J., chairman of the House subcommittee on commerce, transportation and tourism, said that dropping the disclosure requirement in effect tells used car dealers that if they know of a major defect, such as a cracked engine block, they don't have to tell consumers.

Nonetheless, the commission believes that the regulation will help car buyers by making sure they understand the terms and conditions of purchases and by making them wary of promises.

ap 05-08 1:32 pcd

Name _____ Course _____ Date _____

Write a more complete wire story by combining these accounts.

TOKYO (AP) — A U.S. military helicopter with 17 people aboard plunged into the ocean off southern Japan Monday, U.S. military officials said.

Searching ships and planes failed to find survivors, officials said.

Captain Dan Trout, spokesman at the U.S. Kadena Air Base in Okinawa, said it was believed that all 17 aboard the CH-53D helicopter were U.S. Marines.

The downed craft was returning to the Marine base at Futemma, Okinawa, from Iwakuni, another Marine installation in southwest Japan, Trout said.

The helicopter reported mechanical problems and turned back toward Iwakuni, according to Lt. Gary Shrout, spokesman at Yokosuka U.S. Navy Base southwest of Tokyo.

After a few minutes, a second helicopter believed to be traveling on the same route turned to look for the other chopper and spotted an oil slick, Shrout said.

Satoshi Imabayashi of the Maritime Safety Agency, Japan's coast guard, said the second helicopter sighted a man floating in the water with his face down and another clutching a fuel tank, but the second man soon disappeared into the waves.

Trout reported that searches by both American and Japanese aircraft and ships had found no survivors or bodies.

In Washington, Marine spokesman Capt. Mark Hough said the relatives of nine of the 17 missing men had been notified by late Monday.

TOKYO (UPI) — A U.S. Marine helicopter with 17 people aboard crashed in the Pacific off southern Japan Monday, disappearing with only an oil slick left on the ocean surface, American officials said.

Search crews pinpointed the site about 15 miles south-southwest of the island of Yakushima but failed to find any survivors or debris.

The cause of the accident was not immediately known.

"Apparently there were two choppers flying together," Capt. Mark Hough, a Marine Corps spokesman, said in Washington. "The one observed the other go into the water," he said, giving searchers a good fix on the aircraft.

A U.S. military spokesman in Tokyo said an oil slick was spotted at the crash site off the island of Yakushima, but nothing else was found.

The identities of the 17 people who were on board, all military personnel, were withheld pending notification of their relatives, U.S. officials said.

The missing CH-53D helicopter, attached to the 1st Marine Aircraft Wing of the 36th Marine Air Group at Camp Butler in Okinawa, was flying with the other helicopter when it crashed about 625 miles southwest of Tokyo, U.S. officials said in Okinawa and Yokosuka, an American naval base outside Tokyo.

The chopper was flying to Okinawa from the U.S. Marine Corps Air Station at Iwakuni in western Honshu.

U.S. and Japanese patrol ships and aircraft searched the area in a large-scale search that was ordered immediately after reports of the crash, but officials said they failed to locate any survivors.

Hough said the chopper, similar to one President Reagan flies on trips from the White House to the Camp David resort in Maryland, usually carries a three-man crew and is capable of holding up to 38 people.

Name _____ Course _____ Date _____

Write a more complete wire story by combining these accounts.

BEIRUT, Lebanon (AP) — Christian and Moslem gunners battled across the city's dividing line Monday in bloody artillery duels that have claimed dozens of victims in the past week, many of them civilians killed by stray shells.

President Amin Gemayel met with the militia commanders from both sides in an attempt to arrange a cease-fire and a neutral zone between the two parts of the city.

Police reported eight people killed and 53 wounded since Sunday night. That raised the known toll to 37 dead and 240 wounded since the artillery, rocket and mortar battles began April 28.

The demarcation line between the capital's Christian and Moslem sectors has become a wasteland. Even the dogs have gone. The only sign of life is an occasional militiaman, red-eyed and unshaven, slipping from one bit of cover to the next.

The bloodshed, which shows no signs of abating, is accompanied by fears that Gemayel is losing authority among fellow Christians who are split over his pro-Syrian policies.

The fragile coalition government of Moslems and Christians also is split along sectarian lines. It appears helpless, unable even to agree on a place to meet because Cabinet ministers fear to cross into rival territory.

Grim-faced militiamen shoot it out among the shell-blasted buildings of the 3-mile-long "green line" that cuts through the city from north to south.

Moslem fighters were dug in at some points Monday only 10 yards from Christian gunmen facing them from the frontier of the city's eastern sector.

Artillery shells arced into residential districts of both sides, where residents have cowered for days in their basements or in bomb shelters.

Radio stations urged people to stay indoors, but after 10 years of civil war few needed to be told. Many have fled the battle zone for the relative safety to be found a few blocks deeper in their respective districts.

Salvos of rockets fired from multibarreled launchers mounted on trucks cut fiery trails through the sky Sunday night.

BEIRUT, Lebanon (UPI) — Christian and Moslem militiamen battled Monday with rockets, mortars and machine guns in Beirut, killing at least six people and forcing hundreds of civilians to flee their homes.

President Amin Gemayel held emergency talks with army officers on ways to end nine straight days of violence in the Lebanese capital, but the militiamen ignored them and kept on fighting throughout the city.

Scores of rockets and mortar rounds screamed across the city for eight hours, wrecking dozens of homes and parked cars as repeated calls for cease-fires failed and terrified civilians fled for safety.

"The fighters are cowards," said an accountant as his family sat around him in a basement shelter. "They are firing the big guns into areas where they know they will meet no resistance — our homes."

Security sources said two people were killed and 13 wounded in mainly Moslem west Beirut. Four civilians were killed and six wounded in Christian east Beirut in shelling that began in mid-afternoon, nine hours after a cease-fire took effect after heavy fighting overnight.

The latest violence has been heaviest along the Green Line, the 3-mile-long no man's land dividing east and west Beirut.

As fighting raged along the Green Line, gunmen raided a west Beirut theater showing a pornographic movie and forced the all-male audience out to the city's front lines to fill sandbags.

The gunmen, members of a fundamentalist Moslem militia, assailed the moviegoers for "wasting time watching depraved movies," one witness said.

Christian-led army units in east Beirut got involved for the first time since the fighting began April 28, with a spokesman saying the government troops were forced to "answer back and repel attacks" by Moslem gunmen on the Green Line. Twelve soldiers were reported wounded.

The Lebanese Red Cross appealed for all types of blood. Hospital sources said the fighting was so intense that some ambulances were blocked from reaching areas where casualties were reported.

SECTION III

HEADLINE-WRITING SKILLS

Problems

CREATING THE HEADLINE

1. Analyze the headlines on a front page of your local newspaper. How well do they accomplish the purposes of headlines?

2. Take what you consider to be the worst headline on that page and rewrite it, using the same unit count. Explain why your headline is better.

3. Using newspapers available to you, identify and clip out an example of a headline with a kicker, one with a subsidiary deck or dropout, and a hammer head. Tell whether you believe those headline forms were good choices for the stories on which they were used.

4. Read the headlines in an issue of your local newspaper. Then describe whether those headlines were sufficient to serve as an index to the day's news. Why or why not?

AVOIDING HEADLINE PROBLEMS

1. Find three examples of headlines that you believe could be misleading. Using the same counts, rewrite them.

2. Find three headlines that you consider to be inadequate for any reason. Rewrite them as headlines with dropouts. Your instructor will specify the unit counts you must use.

Exercises

Name _____ Course _____ Date _____

Check your ability to determine headline unit counts by listing the counts of each line in the following headlines. Your instructor will specify the counting system to be used.

Fewer farms	_____	Atlanta seeks $1.2 million	_____
to supply most	_____	for youth safety program	_____
of U.S. food	_____		
Doctors report woman	_____	Israel appeals to Syrians	_____
carrying test-tube baby	_____	to remove SAM missiles	_____
Kelley retires	_____	Senate committee	_____
after 31 years	_____	to set conditions	_____
as policeman	_____	for aid to junta	_____
Willie Nelson	_____	Social Security changes	_____
plans concert	_____	may deter bankruptcy	_____
at state prison	_____		

Name _____ Course _____ Date _____

List the key words—those that should be included in the headline—in the following leads.

1. Proposed administration cuts in student aid programs would eliminate more than one million middle-income students from the programs and reduce the aid available to all lower-income students, college and university officials said today.

2. Snipers in Northern Ireland shot and wounded two British soldiers today, and an IRA leader said tensions would "boil over into widespread disorder" unless Britain meets IRA demands.

3. Mayor Rodney Smith said today he will order the city staff to investigate illegal bidding practices in the city purchasing department.

4. A 13-year-old boy was shot to death today as he stepped off a school bus in the northeast part of the city and was hit with a bullet fired by a fleeing bank robber.

5. County Clerk Anne Whitman will ask the county to spend $25,000 for a study of whether voting machines should be purchased next year.

6. Millionaire Ted Turner, creator of the Cable News Network, today filed suit charging the three major networks with antitrust violations and the president and his aides with violating CNN's rights.

7. A local man was admitted Monday to Cooper County Hospital for injuries he sustained in a plane crash during his first solo flight as a student pilot.

8. United States Steel Co. announced price increases today ranging from 8 percent on bar steel, used widely in manufacturing, to 9.7 percent for sheet and strip steel, used extensively in the auto industry.

Name _____ Course _____ Date _____

Write headlines for these stories as specified by your instructor. Do not edit the stories.

1 WHALE

JAMESPORT, N.Y. (UPI) — Physty, the sperm whale who received nationwide publicity when he became beached last month, may have been sighted last week in the Atlantic Ocean about 100 miles off Long Island's south shore.

But the report is unconfirmed, and a marine research biologist said Tuesday he plans to go and look for Physty to make certain of his identity.

"I won't be absolutely sure that Physty is alive and well until we can take photographs of him and compare them with others in our files," said Samuel Sadove of Jamesport.

Sadove, director of the Okeanos Ocean Research Foundation, helped nurse the 12-ton Physty back to health after he was stricken with pneumonia and was found beached near Fire Island April 16.

If the whale turns out to be Physty, it would mark the first time in United States history that a sick whale has been successfully treated and released back into the ocean.

2 EMBASSY

MEXICO CITY (UPI) — Peasants, teachers and students protesting alleged government repression Tuesday peacefully occupied the Swiss, Finnish and Norwegian embassies in Mexico City, police said.

Unarmed female police ejected the protesters from the Finnish mission an hour and 45 minutes after the dissidents seized it and persuaded another band of protestors to leave the Norwegian mission shortly after, police said.

The protesters were unarmed and did not take any hostages, allowing Norwegian Ambassador Jan Arvesen, Swiss Ambassador Rolando Wernuth and Finland's Jussi Montonen to enter and leave their respective missions at will, they said.

The coordinated seizures late Tuesday morning involved nine men and 12 women who took over the Norwegian Embassy, 12 men and a woman at the Finnish mission and five people at the Swiss Embassy, the police said.

The takeovers followed a demonstration at the Interior Ministry in Mexico City where some 10,000 peasants, teachers and students marched on the government office to protest alleged repression in at least 12 Mexican states.

3 BURMA

RANGOON, Burma (UPI) — A massive fire in Mandalay, Burma's second largest city, killed five people, left more than 35,000 homeless and destroyed some 6,000 buildings, reports said Tuesday.

The inferno in the country's ancient royal capital, 430 miles north of Rangoon, broke out late Sunday at a bus terminal in the western part of the city where black market supplies of gasoline were believed hidden.

The fire spread quickly to neighboring buildings and the flames were fed by the 105-degree dry season heat defying firefighters efforts to extinguish the blaze until well after midnight.

Initial reports said more than 35,000 people lost their homes and five people including a child were killed in the fire, one of the worst to hit the country during this year's dry spell.

Over $7 million damage was caused overall with 14 Buddhist monasteries, 10 state-owned schools, seven rice mills, 12 consumer cooperatives and a movie theater burned to the ground.

4 CHECKS

NEW YORK (UPI) — A car containing some $33 million in checks from the European-American Bank was reported stolen Tuesday on Manhattan's lower East Side, but bank officials said the checks were non-negotiable.

"There is absolutely no loss to customers," said Nick Gicas, a spokesman for the bank.

Police said the theft occurred Monday when a messenger for the bank, Robert Kane, returned to find the 1981 blue Pontiac station wagon he had parked in Manhattan, gone.

Kane, 19, was on his way from Westbury, N.Y., where he had picked up the checks, to the bank's processing center on Water Street in Manhattan, police said.

It was not known why Kane had made the stop, but the messenger reported the car stolen to police — apparently unaware of the contents of 15 boxes in the back of the station wagon.

5 TURKEY

ANKARA, Turkey (UPI) — Turkish security forces arrested 243 suspected terrorists in 4 eastern provinces and the western Izmir region, police said Tuesday.

A total of 65 people, including 22 university students, were arrested in Izmir area and all belonged to Dev Yol, a revolutionary leftist group outlawed by Turkish military authorities on charges of seeking a violent overthrow of the military regime.

The group will be charged with 12 assassinations, police said.

In the eastern cities of Erzurum, Kars, Agri and Artvin and surrounding areas, security forces arrested 178 other suspects, including the women, on charges of unspecified killings, bombings, arson and armed robberies, police said.

6 JUSTICE

WASHINGTON (UPI) — The Senate Judiciary Committee today added $109.2 million to a proposed Justice Department authorization bill, boosting the total for fiscal 1982 to $2.4 billion.

The committee postponed until next week a vote on a bill by Chairman Strom Thurmond, R-S.C., to restore the federal death penalty because members wanted to allow more time for what is expected to be extensive debate.

"I support the bill and would like to get it out," Sen. Dennis DeConcini, D-Ariz., told a reporter. "But I wouldn't be surprised if there is a mini-filibuster by those who oppose it."

The committee's Democrats pushed some of the authorization additions to adoption over divided Republicans.

It was understood adjustments may become necessary later if the total exceeds the final limit imposed by the Senate Budget Committee, but a committee staff member said there was an allowable margin for some increases.

Printed by permission of United Press International.

Write headlines for these stories as specified by your instructor. Do not edit the stories.

1 MUGABE

PEKING (UPI) — Prime Minister Robert Mugabe of Zimbabwe, who received Chinese support during a guerrilla war against Rhodesia's white government, arrived in Peking Tuesday on a five-day official visit.

African diplomats expect Mugabe to ask for Chinese economic and perhaps military assistance to help his struggling nation overcome internal and external problems.

2 WHIRL

GENOA, Italy (UPI) — A whirlwind whipped through the outskirts of this northwest coastal city early Tuesday, damaging houses, cars and boats, police said.

Police said the Genoa-Savona train line was closed for several hours because the wind blew debris on power lines.

3 PLUNGE

NEW DELHI, India (UPI) — A bus plunged into a canal in the northern state of Kashmir Tuesdau, killing three people and injuring 31 others, the Press Trust of India reported.

The accident occurred near Akhnoor town, close to the Pakistani border, about 400 miles northwest of New Delhi.

4 AID

GENEVA, Swizterland (UPI) — The United States joined other nations in pledging a total aid package worth $21 million for drought and flood victims in China, the United Nations said Tuesday.

An appeal for aid was launched by the U. N. Disaster Relief Organization on March 23 for victims of drought in the Hebei province and flood victims in Hubei province. It was the first time that China had requested U.N. assistance.

5 INDICT

KANSAS CITY, Kan. (UPI) — A federal grand jury has indicted five members of a Great Bend family for allegedly failing to report nearly $600,000 found stuffed into suitcases in the home of a deceased relative.

U.S. Attorney James Buchele said the two-count indictment, released Monday, could signal "the largest tax fraud case in Kansas history."

After the death of dentist Kenneth A. Mitchell, his relatives allegedly reported to the Internal Revenue Service that only $282,035 was found in the basement of Mitchell's home, when $859,785 was allegedly discovered.

Buchele said the tax on the allegedly unreported money could be $200,000, but a conviction for attempting to defraud the federal government of estate tax could result in an additional 50 percent penalty tax.

The elder Mitchell died Dec. 21, 1976, and left his cash — in bills all smaller than $100 — in several suitcases hidden in the basement because he didn't believe in banks.

Named in the indictment were Mitchell's widow, Lorraine E. Mitchell; his son, Kenneth E. Mitchell; his dauther, Melinda Heinz; his brother, Lawrence C. Mitchell, and daughter-in-law, Louise Mitchell.

6 CHINA

PEKING (UPI) — China's first English-language newspaper since the 1949 Communist takeover will begin daily publication on June 1, publisher Jiang Muyao said Tuesday.

The China Daily has been printing trial issues three times a week and has built up a circulation of 18,000 copies per day.

The newspaper will be distributed in Peking, Shanghai, Canton, Xian, Hangzhou and other cities, particularly those with large numbers of foreigners.

The newspaper, which covers both international and Chinese news, costs less than 10 cents on newsstands.

7 SCALD

NEW YORK (UPI) — A cleaning woman in a midtown office building was scalded to death Tuesday when a steam pipe valve burst releasing a powerful blast of super-hot steam, authorities said.

A spokesman for Con Edison said the steam spread through the Diamond International Building on Third Avenue and turned it into a 24-story sweatbox.

The temperature of the steam was estimated to be in "excess of 212 degrees."

"The stairwells were just like chimneys for the steam," said one firefighter, soaking wet from the hot steam and sweat. "The thing about steam is that you can't escape it."

The dead woman was identified as Carmen Ballesta, 47, of Queens. She was changing out of her uniform at the time of the blast, a few minutes after midnight.

Police said 17 other maintenance workers escaped injury when they made their way to the upper floors and were rescued by 50 firefighters.

8 TRANSPLANT

LONDON (UPI) — Doctors successfully transplanted the heart of a 13-year-old girl in a 51-year-old man and left his heart in place during a four-hour operation Sunday at Harefield Hospital, a spokesman said Tuesday.

It was the first "piggy back" transplant performed in Britain. The technique of placing the transplant heart side by side with a patient's own heart was developed by South African surgeon Dr. Christian Barnard.

Peter Scott was in stable condition following the operation, doctors said.

The girl was killed in a traffic accident.

9 SAUDI

RIYADH (UPI) — King Khaled of Saudi Arabia Tuesday ordered $10 million in food and clothing be sent to flood victims in Somalia and South Yemen, the Gulf News Agency said.

Edit this story and write a headline as specified by your instructor.

Overpass

The days of the dangerous Route WW-U.S. Highway 63 South intersection are over.

Fred Kosnan, Highway Dept. resident engineer, said the Route WW overpass over Highway 63 on the east edge of the city opened today.

The overpass, part of a widening project on U.S. 63 S., is located just north of the highway's old intersection with Route WW.

Konsnan, said signs directing drivers to the overpass will be posted and he urged drivers to use caution in the area. The old intersection was considered one of the state's most dangerous.

—30—

Name _____ **Course** _____ **Date** _____

Edit this story and write a headline as specified by your instructor.

BLOOD

A Red Cross community blood drive will be held Tuesday from 1 p.m. to 6 p.m. at the Kelley Motor Spectrum, 500 Vandiver Drive.

To ensure an adequate blood supply for hospitalized patients all healthy residents are encouraged to danote.

Red Cross supplies all blood used by patients in 140 hospitals, including the hospitals serving the city. The agency collects 900 units of blood every day to give to accident victims, new mothers, cancer patients and others.

Donors must be between the ages of 17 and 65, weigh 105 pounds and have no record of heart disease, cancer or hepatitis.

-30-

Name _____ Course _____ Date _____

Edit this story and write a headline as specified by your instructor.

GENETICS

 The 17th Stadler Genetics Symposium will be held at the University today and Tuesday. The symposium will focus on genetic development and evolution through 16 presentations by internationally recognized scientists.

 The University's Middlebush Auditorium is the site for all speakers' presetations. The talks will run from 8 a.m. to 5 p.m. today, and 8 a.m. to 5 p.m. Tuesday. Speakers include Nobel Laureate G.M. Edelman of Rockefeller University in New York and world-famous plant geneticist G.L. Stebbins of the University of California--Davis.

 Registration will be held from 7 to 8 a.m. today at Middlebush Auditorium.

-30-

Name _____ Course _____ Date _____
_____

Edit this story and write a headline as specified by your instructor.

ASSAULT

     Gerald W. Hartman, 58, 2100 W. Broadway, reported to police that he and two other people were assaulted early on Tuesday morning by two men. One of the assailants had a revolver.

     Hartman told police that the two men followed him into his residence and asked if they could use his phone.

     Hesaid they followed him to the kitchen where one of the men pulled out a short barrelled revolver and pointed it at him.

     The men forced Hartman, Edward McDaniels, 51, 1305 Golf Boulevard, and an inidentified woman into an upstairs bedroom and "roughed them up a bit," according to a police spokesman.

     The two men looked around the house for something, he said, while he and the two persons, who were visiting him, stayed in the bedroom.

     One of the men was described as black, 5 feet 8, 150 pounds with a moustache, police reported.

—30—

Name _____ Course _____ Date _____

Edit this story and write a headline as specified by your instructor.

P&Z

      The Planning and Zoning Commission tomorrow will consider an application to construct a plant to manufacture cement at a quarry near the Municipal Golf Course.

      Peter Davis, the chairman of the commission, said Harold Johnson has asked the property to be rezoned from agricultural to general industrial. The request calls for 11 acres of the 165-acre property to be rezoned. The city staff has recommended approval.

      The commission also will consider an application by Westenhaver Construction, Incorporated, to build a planned unit development containing 37 single-family units, 15 duplex units and seven four-plex units. The sight is on Green Meadows Road overlooking Hinkson creek.

      Paul W. Dieckmann has applied to rezone 25 acres on Rt. E from agricultural use to medium density apartments.

      The commission also will consider revising the city's parking ordinance to permit parking on lawns during university football games. The city council Tuesday night referred the issue to the commission for a recommendation.

—30—

Edit this story and write a headline as specified by your instructor.

boy

    A seven-year-old local boy was trapped Sunday in an air pocket of a capsized boat for forty-five minutes on Clear Lake.

    Steve Mermelstein, 2009 Sappington Dr., was on a 36-foot aluminum bouseboat, owned by Beryl Ortwerth, Crescent Meadows Trailer Ct., that overturned in 65 to 75 mile an hour winds during a rainstrom on the Gravois Arm of the lake, according to the state water patrol.

    Steve was inside of the main cabin when the boat overturned. Bouyed by his life preserver, he floated to the top of the boat where air was trapped, said officer Joe Penrod.

    45 minutes passed before he was rescued by Jack Wilcox and Al Hall, 2 employees of Paige's Boat Yard, Penrod said. Wilcox dove into the water and swam inside the main cabin, groping for the boy because it was too dark to see, the water patrol said.

    "We expected him to be dead, but when I touched him, I could feel him moving," Wilcox said. When I returned to the surface, I shouted "He's alive!"

    Steve was taken to a Milan clinic, where he was treated for minor bruises and shock and released.

—30—

Edit this story and write a headline as specified by your instructor.

SLASH

By JAMES AXOLOTL
Staff Writer

Midway Heights School District students will go back to school tomorrow after punctured tires on their school busses kept them home today.

"We'll be able to get all the tires fixed today," District Superintendant Mel Cowznofsky said. "All 24 tires will be okay for Wednesday."

The busses were parked at a service station when the puncturing incident occurred some time over the week-end. One or more vandals damaged 10 front and 14 rear tires on four of the district's five buses.

The vandalism was discovered this morning.

"Evidently, it was done with a pocket knife or something with a thin blade," Boone Co. Sherriff Charles Foster said. "The tires don't appear to be slashed. Whoever did it just punctured them."

MORE

SLASH-first add

The sheriff's department has been investigating the incident, but has made little progress.

"We don't have any leads right now," Foster said this afternoon. "I have a man in the Midway vicinity working on it, but he hasn't reported back to me yet. I don't think much has been accomplished."

The damage was estimated at $30,00 to $5,000.

—30—

Name _____ Course _____ Date _____

Edit this story and write a headline as specified by your instructor.

Mistrial

   A mistrial was declared Tuesday in Boone County Circuit court in the 1st degree robbery trial of James T. Campbell. The mistrial was declared after a police officer indicated, while on the witness stand, that Campbell had a prior police record.

   Campbell, 20, of Cincinnati, Ohio is charged with robbing Dean Edmonson, of Fairfield, Washington, while Edmonson was hitchhiking along Interstate 70 on July 2. Travelers checks were taken in the robbery.

   Judge John Cave declared the mistrial during the testimony of Paul Neal, a police detctive. Neal said that Campbell had asked to speak with his parole officer while being questioned by Boone County Prosecuting. Atty. Joe Moseley.

   Neal's statement indicated Campbell has a police record. Under state law, evidence of a previous record of arrest and conviction cannot be presented in court unless the defendent appears on the witness stand. Campbell has not testified in the trial.

   Assistant public Defender Dave Doak, Campbell's attorney, said the trial would be rescheduled, probably for next month.

MORE

MISTRIAL--first add

Just previous to the trial, Attorney Doak requested the case be dismissed because, he said, Moseley had asked for an improper physical examination of Campbell on Sunday evening. Cave denied the dismissal request.

While reviewing the case, Moseley bacame curious about some tatoos he thought Campbell had, according to testimony. Moseley called the jail to check. Doal contended that Harper violated Campbell's right to have an attorney present during an examination.

—30—

Edit this story and write a headline as specified by your instructor.

CREDIT

Mastercard is welcome at the County Jail. So is Visa.

People may now use bank cards to post bond at the jail under a program started this week. Lt. Lyn Woolford, commander of the services division, said the only restriction is that the card cover the amount of bond.

Sheriff Ted Boehm said that so far only one person has taken advantage of the option, posting a $250 bond on a charge of driving while under suspension or revocation.

Woolford said people are informed of the option when they do not have enough cash to cover their bond. A sign advertising the option is posted at the jail. If they don't own a card, they can ask friends to bail them out with a credit card.

Woolford said people haven't been taking advantage of the option because they don't have cards or don't want to put bond on their card.

If they do opt for plastic, the sheriff's office calls a toll-free number to ensure that the cards have not been stolen and that the holder's have enough credit.

more

CREDIT--first add

Boehm said that if more people used credit cards, the jail would be less crowded.

People brought in late at night often do not have enough cash to post bond, he said. They have to call friends wh might not arrive for a couple of hours or might have to wait until the banks open the next morning.

The sheriff's office has to go through the time-consuming process of incarcerating them although they will be getting out on bond as soon as the cash becomes available, Boehm said.

Woolford does not feel that the program is unfair to those who do not own credit cards.

"It's just another option for those who have cards," he said.

A subcommittee of the County Facilities Commission suggested last September that the County Commission study the possibility of using credit cards to post bond. The commission approved, budgeting $2,000 on Jan. 10 for the effort, according to County Clerk Wendy Noren.

The county will use the money to pay a monthly fee of 2 percent of the bonds charged to the credit card companies.

Northern District Commissioner Alex Gates said the option is intended for use be people charged with traffic offenses.

Boehm likes the idea. "We use credit cards for everything. Why not for posting bond - as long as the credit is good.

-30-

Edit this story and write a headline as specified by your instructor.

BOOT

By Fern W. Good
Staff reporter

If you haven't been paying your parking tickets, it is quite possible that you'll find your auto immobilized by a 23-lb. metal device called a "boot" that clamps on the left front tire of a vehicle.

The City has been considering its use for about 2 months and soon will order one that is expected to arrive next month. Bob Black, assistant to the city manager, said that if the boot works as is hoped, two more will probably be bought.

An ordnance to allow use of the boots will be presented to the city council Monday and will be voted on next month. Each boot costs $300.

Meter Maids carry lists of people who have five or more tickets that are not paid. If the ordnance is passed, when meter maids observe a car on the list, they will check with the City Court to confirm that the person has not recently paid the tickets.

If the tickets haven't been paid, the boot will be placed on the tire, immobilizing the car. A note will put on the wind-

MORE

BOOT -- first add

shield saying damage could result if an attempt is made to move the car.

If the vehicle is not claimed and the tickets are paid within 24 hours, the car will be towed.

Police Chief Dave Walsh said he initiated the move to purchase the boots for several reasons. Citizens would not be forced to pay towing and impoundment fees and police manpower would be saved by eliminating the need to have an officer present when a car is towed. Walsh said the boots also would serve as advertisement the the city is taking action against unpaid tickets because they will be brightly painted and obvious to passerby.

There are 162 persons who have five or more unpaid tickets in Columbia. The present record holder is Lynda Kruse, who has been issued 55 tickets and faces a minimum find of at least $275. She has since moved out of town.

—30—

Name _____ Course _____ Date _____
_____

Edit this story and write a headline as specified by your instructor.

Aly obit

    Bower Aly, 84, a retierd University speech professor, once honored by ex-President Lindon B. Johnson as the "Father of High School Debate," died Sept. 10 in Eugene, Oregon where he had been hospitalaized for a period of about two months.

    A mainstay on the university Speech Department faculty for nearly 3 decades, Aly served as presidnt of the Speech Communication Assn. in 1944 and later as editor of it's "Quarterly Journal of speech."

    Aly's dedication to the field of speech communication earned a letter from Johnson some time in 1966. "You have contributed much in helping thousands of young men and women learn to use their minds, the letter said.

    Mr. Aly was born in Crystal City in 1903. He was a university faculty member from 1930 to 1957 and a visiting professor at Columbia University, the University of Wisconsin and the Collge of the City of New York. During the time he was at the university of Hawaii, he helped establish a Speech Department.

    In 1973 Aly retired from the University of Oregon after teaching there for sixteen years.

                                    more

Aly obit - first aid

    Considered a leading authority on debate, Mr. Aly for more than thirty years was editor of the "Discussion and Debate Manual, a university extension publication used in colleges and secondary scholls.

    Mr. Aly also wrote two books, "An Inventory of the library of Congress Collection of Texts and american Speeches" and "The Rhetoric of Alexander Hamilton."

    He received a B.A. from Southwest State College in 1925, an M.A. from the University in 1926 and a PH. D. from Columbia University in 1941.

    Mr. Aly is survived by his widow, Lucile, Eugene; three sons, Robert Aly, Lawrence, Kans., Tom Aly, 2367 Ridge Boulevard, and Willaim Aly, Eugene, and two grandchildren.

    A graveside service was officiated by Rev. Bob Johnson of New Haven on Sept. 14 at the Fulton Cemetary. A memorial service also was held in Eugene, Ore.

—30—

Name _____ Course _____ Date _____

Edit this story and write a headline as specified by your instructor.

hospital

    Maintainance workers at Elis Fischel State Cancer hospital may have been exposed to undertermined amounts of radiation in the shop area because they were unaware that safety precautions should have been taken.

    The employes work in a room that is located right underneath a room containing an ortho voltage x-ray treatment machine. Warning lites in the work room signal ocuppants to leave when the X-ray machine is operating, but workers say they never realized what the lights were there for.

    The workers, mostly elctricians, plumbers and cabinet makers say they had heard "rumors" or "informal talk" about such rules, but had never sene any written guidelines during the 2 years they had worked in the area.

    "Most of us never payed any attention to the lights because all we had ever heard was rumors, said John Smith, a Hospital worker for four years who has worked in the room under suspicion for a year. "None of us ever took them seriously since we'd never seen anything on paper."

                                             more

hospital-first add

The lights were installed when the hospital was built in 1940. The work room was used for storage until two years ago. About twelve workers became concerned about possible radiation exposure when another area in the hospital was routinely checked fro radiation about three weeks ago.

At the worker's request hospital radiation safety officer Clifford Richey checked the area and sent a report to the workers and hospital administrator Virgil Yates. It was the first radiaton survey in the area since 1973.

Smith said, "There was no communication between us and Richey when the report was finished. He sent us figures we didn't understand and didn't come to us to explain them."

Richey was unavalable for comment.

After Richey's report workers asked Yates to request a test from the state Bureau of Radiological Health. That test was made Monday.

Yates said the people "who worked in the store room were aware of the procedure and had become accustomed to it. The problem came when the area was changed from a storeroom to a work room."

—30—

Edit this story and write a headline as specified by your instructor.

SAFETY

Union Electric Co. officials said Saturday there are no safety-related problems at its Callaway Nuclear Plant, despite recent disclosures that fifteen quality-control inspectors may not have proper centification.

Seven inspector's certifications were in doubt last month. Fifteen have now been added to the original seven, for a total of 22 as of Friday.

UE officials recently investigated 60 quality-control inspectors' certifications, and of these 60, fifteen were found with certifications in doubt, Mike Cleary said. Cleary is supervisor of nuclear information at the plant.

The plant's management ordered a review last month of about 12,000 workorders because a UE investigation found that seven of its quality-control inspectors performed some duties for which there qualifications were in doubt.

"We expect the entire review of the 12,000 word orders and there re lation to the 22 inspectors to be finished by the second week of April," Cleary said.

(more)

SAFETY-first add

    Since 1983, 12,000 workorders have been served at the plant. The orders were completed by construction workers contracted by Daniel Interantional, the firm which built the plant. Daniel international inspected its construction of the plant.

    The operational safety of the completed construction was then checked by the UE quality-control inspectors. The UE review is related to these inspectors and their faze in plant operations, and is not related to the construction of theplant, Bob Powers said. Powers is an assistant manager of quality assurance for the plant.

    Cleary said, "Of the work requests reviewed as of Friday, three percent involved work wherequality-control inspectors' qualifications were in doubt.

    "Of this three per cent there have been no safety concerns about the inspections."

    The primary concern of plant officials is safety, Cleary said. "We are making sure that the safety of the systems at the plant are not in question. There has been no need to re-inspect any of the work orders reviewed so far."

                                             -30-

Edit this story and write a headline as specified by your instructor.

DEAD

By MILES ARCHER
Staff Writer

A Miami, Fla., woman on her way home was discovered dead earlier today when the car she was riding in stopped at a local service station.

A Boone County Medical Examiner said preliminary results of an autopsy showing the exact cause of death will be ready tomorrow.

According to a police report, Sallie Lancaster, 22, was in the back seat of the car at 5 a.m. this morning when she told the driver, Fred Mertz, 60, that she did not feel well and was going to take some pills to enable her to sleep for awhile.

When Mertz, Long Beach, Mississippi, had heater trouble near here at about 7:30 a.m., he stopped at the Interstate 70 Shell service station, 1004 Stadium Blvd. When he tried to wake up Miss Lancaster, he found her dead.

Results of a blood and urine tests from an autopsy done on Miss Lancaster's body this afternoon are needed to show the cause of death, according to Dr. Perry Oskins, one of four Boone County coroners.

more

DEAD -- first add

The tests, which will be completed by the end of the week, would show if chemical substances were in Miss Lancaster's bloodstream. Police contacted Miss Lancaster's physician in suburban Coconut Grove, who said he gave her a prescription for tranquilizers, according to Oskins.

Police said that Mertz had run an advertisement in a Miami newspaper, looking for riders to share traveling expenses to Denver.

Miss Lancaster answered the ad, and the two left Miami last week in Mertz's Rambler, police said. Mertz reportedly dropped Miss Lancaster off in Denver before driving on to Aspen, Col.

Police said Mertz picked up Miss Lancaster yesterday afternoon in Denver. The two reportedly were on their way back to Florida when Mertz stopped here.

—30—

Edit this story and write a headline as specified by your instructor.

IDA

The Industrial Development Authority gave preliminary approval Tuesday for bond financing to two applicants, one to expand an existing business and another to create a new storage complex.

The authority, with only four of sevne members present gave unanimous approval in little more than an hour to Richard and Rose Ditter to expand D Sport Shop, a sporting goods store at 1034 E. Walnut St., and to Lawrence Bulgin to construct a storage facility and office complex off Worley Street.

Bulgin, who owns Bulgin Development Co. at 301 Vieux Carre Court, was given approval for about $1.9 million in revenue bonds to build commercial office spane and to provide city residents and businesses with self-storage facilities.

The authority approved Richard Ditter's D Sprot application for $500,000 in revenue bonds to renovate the shop's existing building and to all about 5,000 square feet for retail sales and display to the shop.

Tuesday's approval is only the first step in receiving the funding. The two owners must now try to find bond buyers for more than $2.4 million in industrial revenue bonds. The

(more)

IDA-first add

owners will receive final approval from the authority when bvnd purchasing arrangements are made.

If given final approval, Bulgin's proposal will create 19,572 square feet of office space and 42,500 square feet of storage structures to be leased on an 5.81-acre tract. The complex will serve as a "support facility" for the two mall developments.

Michael Bathke, a city planning consultant, said even if Bulgin builds on the tract, located west of the shopping mall on the south side of Worley Street, the area would be "just about as invisible as it is now."

Lawrence and Jacqueline Bulgin may incorporate their enterprise as a proprietorship called Centre West Office and Storage Park. The proposed 21-building development would be their first office and storage park. Construction would begin 90 days after bond funding is available, according to the authority application.

Ditter, who started D Sport in 1977, said the building he now owns is "an eyesore" in the downtown area. Ditter said he would remodel and add to the shop's interior, using the existing building for storage. He also plans to use a lot owned by him and Rose Ditter. Rose Ditter owns Kelani's Hair Inc., 1104 E. Walnut St. The lot, between the sporting goods store and the hair shop, is used for parking

(more)

IDA-second add

    The store extension qualifies for bond financing, Ditter said, because he is renovating an old building, doubling his employment staff from 15 to 30 employees and increasing the downtown property value by adding building space.

-30-

Edit this story and write a headline as specified by your instructor.

BROWN

With less that two weeks to go before the April 2 election, Nate Brown withdrew his condidacy, leaving Sharon Lynch and the Rev. Raymond Prince to battle in what is now a one-on-one race for the Sixth Ward City Council Seat.

Brown announced his withdrawal and gave his support to Lynch at a Friday meeting of the Pachyderms, a local Repblican club. Despite Brown's endorsement choice, Prince said that the outcome of the race will not be effected.

"We always thought that Mrs. Lynch was the one to beat," Prince said. "We never did consider Nate Brown a threat. The people who were going to vote for him are still up in the air, and it's up to us to go get them. We still think we have a good chance to win."

Although Lynch, 34, is grateful for Brown's endorsement, she is cautiuos about how much influence it will have on the race's outcome. Like Prince, she said she will have to go out and campaign for that vote.

(more)

Brown-first add

"Just because Brown has siad he supports me and will encourage his supporters to vote for me, I cannot assume they will. I still have to earn their vote. If Nate and I share the same views on some of the issues, then hopefully that would sway some of his supporters to vote for me."

With Brown's abrupt withdrawal, speculation surfaced that council contenders are playing party politics in a non-partisan race.

But Brown, 26, said that being a Republican had nothing to do with his decision to endorse Lynch. "She's not a Republican," he said. "I think she's an independent. Anyway, I gave her my support because we share common ground."

Lynch and Prince seem to agree on at least one thing: They both say that the City Council race is non-partisan and that their views refect issues not party affiliation.

"I am not a Republican or a Democrat," Lynch said. "I am registered to vote, but I vote for the person and the issue."

Prince, 30, has said thaty Lynch and Brown have tried to label him a liberal. "Labels like 'conservative and 'liberal' ahve no place in local politics," he said. "I have conservative views on some issues and liberal views on others."

(more)

Brown-second add

Brown, a special sections coordinator for a local newspaper, cited work obligations and a "crippled campaign" as the reasons for withdrawing from the race.

He also was unable to canvas the sixth Ward and meet other campaign obligations because of time constraints due to his job.

Brown blamed Shelia Sweeney, his volunteer campaign manager, for failing in her responsibility to run his campaign. He said the last time he saw or heard from her was on March 5.

"It was her responsibility," Brown said. "She was not working, not goint to school - all she had to do was run my campaign. She started but she didn't finish. When the campaign structure started to fall apart, there was no way to recover."

Although he was unable to contact Sweeney for three weeks, Brown made no effort to repair his failing campaign. After efforts to find Sweeney failed, Brown did not seek a replacement. When asked why, he said: "We've dropped out of the campaign. We've given our reasons, and that's that."

In addition to Sweeney's unexplained disappearance, Brown's campaign treasurer Charlie Roemer quit.

Prince said Brown left the campaign "obviously because he felt he could not run against us."

"Shelia isn't the one who was running," Prince said. "When I got into the race, I knew what my schedule was. If I didn't have the time, I wouldn't have gotten into it. He should have known that.

-30-

Edit this story and write a headline as specified by your instructor.

NEGLECT

Some of the more powerful members of the state judicial and legislative systems are pushing a program to help abused and neglected children.

More than 100 Missouri judges, social workers and juvenile officers, including Supreme Court Justice Andrew Higgins, are attending a conference here to discuss ways to monitor abused and neglected children who may become "lost" in foster homes.

"What happens across the country is that the children are placed in temporary foster care and then forgotten by the court system," says Bob Pratski, project director for the National Council of Junvile and Family Court Judges. "The children grow up without family ties and drift from home to home."

The conference, which ends Tuedsday, will primarily focus on the Court Appointed Special Advocate, or CASA, program.

The CASA "is the eyes and ears of the court when dealing with abused or neglected children thar pulled out of their homes by the court," Carmen Ray says. "The CASA is the conscience of society to protect our children."

(more)

Neglect-first add

Ray serves as executive director of the National Court Appointed Special Advocate Association. She started the organization in 1977 to help keep track of children in a court system where one judge hears thousands of cases.

The conference is at the Ramada Inn, 1100 Vandiver Drive. State Rep. Kaye Steinmetz, D-Springfield will speak today.

The CASA deals with children who are victims of problems which are as much an issue locally as nationally, Local police investigated 21 cases of sexual abuse of children in 1984. But many more crimes go unreported. National studies indicate that before reaching 18 years of age, half of all girls and 10 percent of all boys will be sexually abused by an audlt, the Associated Press recently reported.

Most child molesters are related to the child or the family, police say. Fathers, stepfathers and boyfriends of the mother, in that order, account for the highest percentage of abuse, says Dective Susal Stoltz of the Police Department.

Those abused or neglected children who reach the court system may move from foster home to foster home. "Each time a child is moved, they're damaged, leading the kids to the street and the crimes associated with the street, such as drugs and prostitution," Ray says.

Chief Justice Higgins agrees. "One of the premises of planned permanecy (a permanent home system) is that an abused

(more)

Neglect-second add

or neglected child will become a law-violator and perhaps a child abuser as an adult."

In the CASA program one volunteer is assigned as a courtroom advocate to each abused or neglected child. "The CASA can exclusively focus attention on the child's best interest," Ray says.

The CASA, who is trained by other volunteers, becomes familiar with all parties involved with an abused child - the child, parents and foster parents. The CASA then reports relevant facts to the court and monitors the child's situation until the child returns home or is placed in a permanent home.

CASAs are carefully screened and recruited. Ray says, "The courts are looking for a person who has the ability ot handle informati n and form an independent position that's not influenced by the judges, case workers or attorneys.

"CASAs have to have the courage to stand up in court to voice their opinions," she says.

There are 150 jurisdictions across the country that use the CASA system. Our state, with eight jurisdictions using CASA, "is on the cutting edge of what the National CASA association is trying to do," Pratski says.

Pratski and Higgins are quick to point out that CASAs are not social workers. Higgins says that arguments that the system burdens the courts with paper work and administrative costs are unfounded.

(more)

Neglect-third add

"Since the workers themselves are volunteer, there is not much more than underwriting for the administrative process and some expense for the process of monitoring...," he said. "You always have to deal with the problem that any new idea has in gaining acceptance. We are pretty successful in persuading."

The event is being co-sponsored by the National Court Appointed Special Advocate Association and the National Council of Juvenile and Family Court Judges Association.

-30-

SECTION IV

PICTURES, GRAPHICS, AND DESIGN

Problems

PICTURE EDITING

1. Find an example of a picture you believe your newspaper should not have used. On what is your opinion based? Defend your position.

2. You are working as news editor of a paper in Williamsburg, Va. You must decide whether to publish the fire tragedy pictures shown in the textbook (Figures 12-10a and 12-10b). What is your decision? Defend your position.

3. As news editor of the Williamsburg paper, once again you are confronted with a decision about whether to publish pictures of a tragedy. This time the picture shows the mangled body of a local woman killed in a traffic accident. She was well known in the community for her civic work. Would you publish the picture? Why or why not?

4. The wire services have transmitted a picture of the vice president making an obscene gesture to hecklers during a speech. Should you publish the picture? Why or why not?

AN INTRODUCTION TO TYPE

1. Your publisher has asked you to suggest a typeface to be used for headlines. Her instructions are to select a face that reflects the history of your newspaper as an old, reliable publication. Suggest three typefaces and defend your choices.

2. Inspect the body type of two newspapers you read regularly. Identify the typefaces and tell which one you think is more legible. Explain your position.

3. Find an example of poor spacing in a newspaper. Explain what you would have done to eliminate the problem.

4. You are the news editor of your local newspaper, which is planning to install a pagination system. The computer company has asked you to list specifications for spacing within the newspaper. List all the important spacing standards, such as space between columns, horizontal space between stories, and so forth.

FUNDAMENTALS OF NEWSPAPER DESIGN

1. Describe, in your own words, the purposes of newspaper design.

2. Take a front page from your local newspaper and describe how the layout artist or designer has used the principles of artistic design.

3. Using copies of three newspapers to which you have access, describe the makeup concepts involved. Would you consider them to be traditional or contemporary?

4. Take a copy of a page that you consider to be poorly designed. Rework the page using the same elements.

CONTEMPORARY MAKEUP AND DESIGN PRACTICES

1. Clip from available newspapers examples of contemporary headline placement. Are the stories enhanced by such special treatment?

2. Check three newspapers in your area to see how jumps are handled. Are they easy to find? If not, what could be done to help the reader find them?

MAKEUP OF SPECIAL PAGES

1. Find three newspaper front pages. Which one best employs the principle of artistic dominance?

2. Using the checklist in Chapter 16 of the textbook, rate the three front pages you selected for Question 1.

Exercises

Name _____ Course _____ Date _____

_____

Crop these pictures as you see fit. Then size them according to instructions provided by your instructor and prepare a layout for the story and pictures. Finally, write cutlines from the caption information provided by the photographer.

Photo Caption

Hanging On

Photographer
Brian Lincoln

Date
May 12

Department
News

Ordered by:
Enterprise

Approved: D. P.

Caption Information
10-months-old Drew Blindell keeps a tight grip on his father's hair at the Home Show Tuesday at the Fairgrounds Arena. Dad, Lonnie Blindell of 1034 Parker St., was registering for a door prize.

Location
Fairgrounds Arena

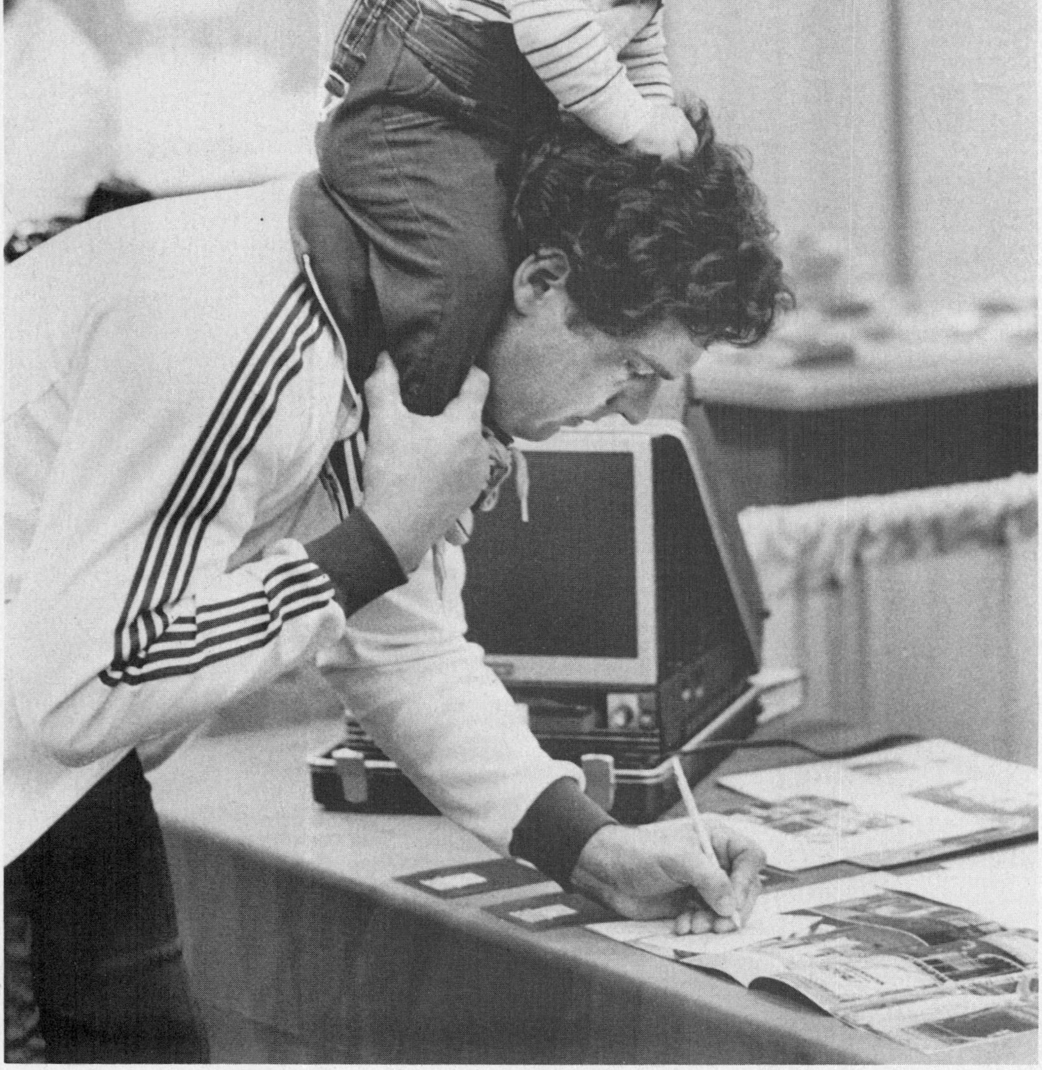

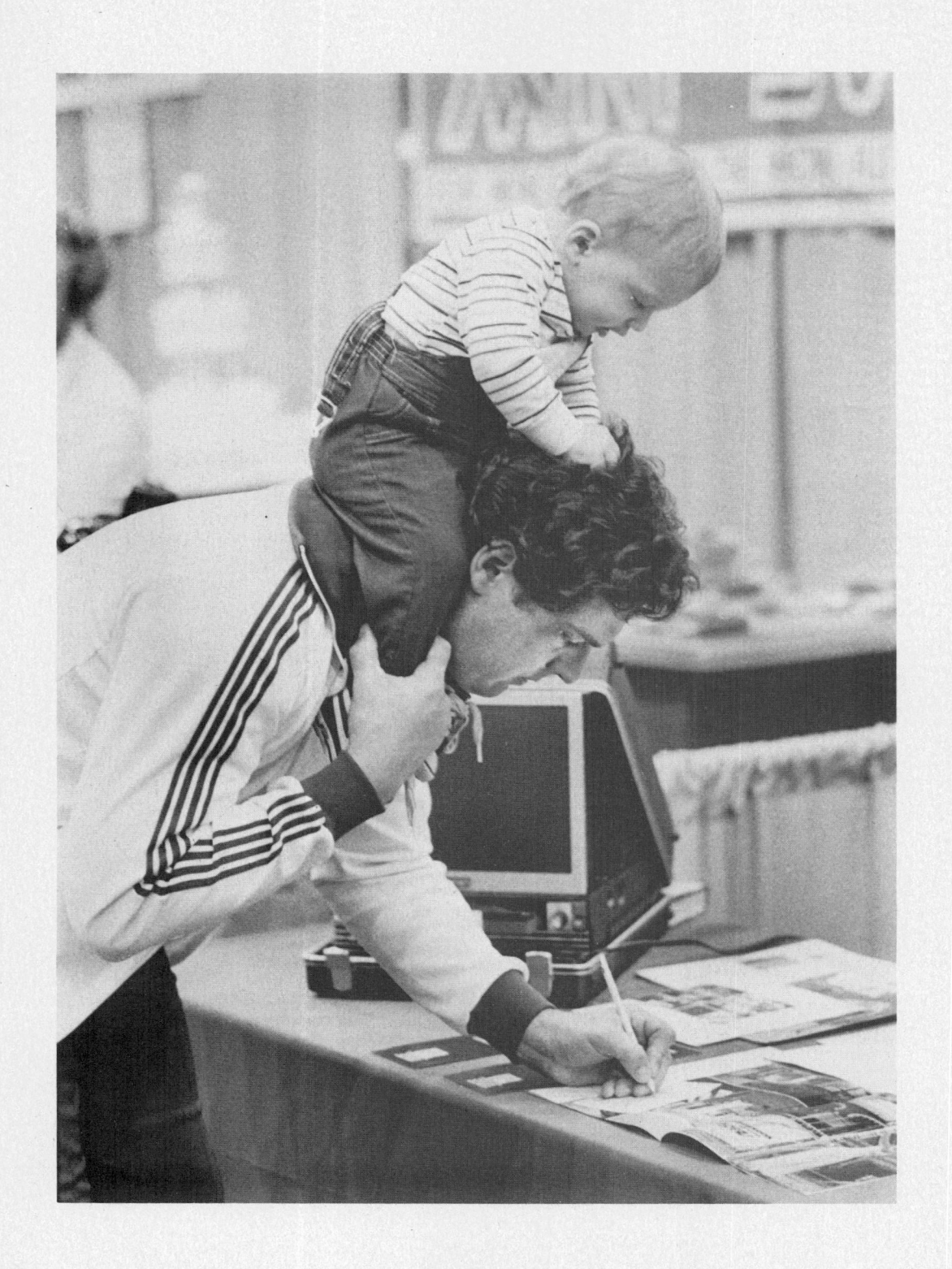

Name _____ Course _____ Date _____

_____

Crop this picture as you see fit. Then size it according to instructions provided by your instructor. Finally, write a cutline from the caption information provided by the photographer.

Photo Caption

Photographer
Leon Portillo

Date
Nov. 11

Department
News

Ordered by:
Enterprise

Approved: B.K.

Caption Information

Two unidentified canoe enthusiasts took to the waters Friday for a paddle up the Missouri River near Easley. They had plenty of beer to make the day enjoyable and the weather was unseasonably warm. The temperature was 65 degrees.

Location
Missouri River near Easley

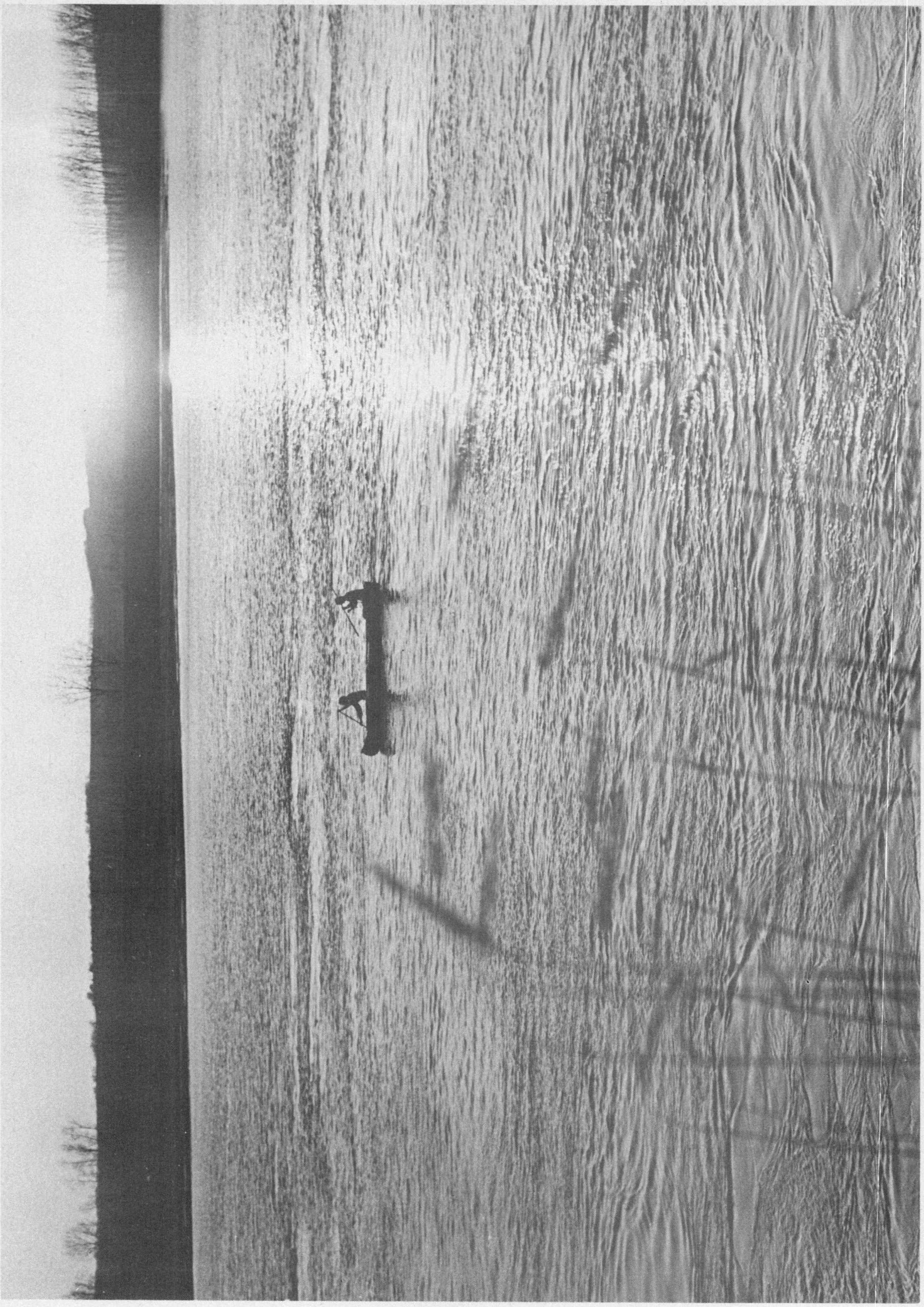

Name _____ Course _____ Date _____

_____

Crop this picture as you see fit. Then size it according to instructions provided by your instructor. Finally, write a cutline from the caption information provided by the photographer.

Photo Caption

Photographer
Ann Lively

Date
Sept. 3

Department
News

Ordered by:
City Desk

Approved: B.K.

Caption Information

The Mehlville Horse Show is just a week away, so Melanie Grover is busy trying to convince her horse, Red Delight, to jump fences. Red and Melanie will jump in the show, which will begin at 7 p.m. Sept. 10. Admission is $2 for adults and $1 for children at the Mehlville Arena. Horses get in free.

Location
Mehlville Fairgrounds

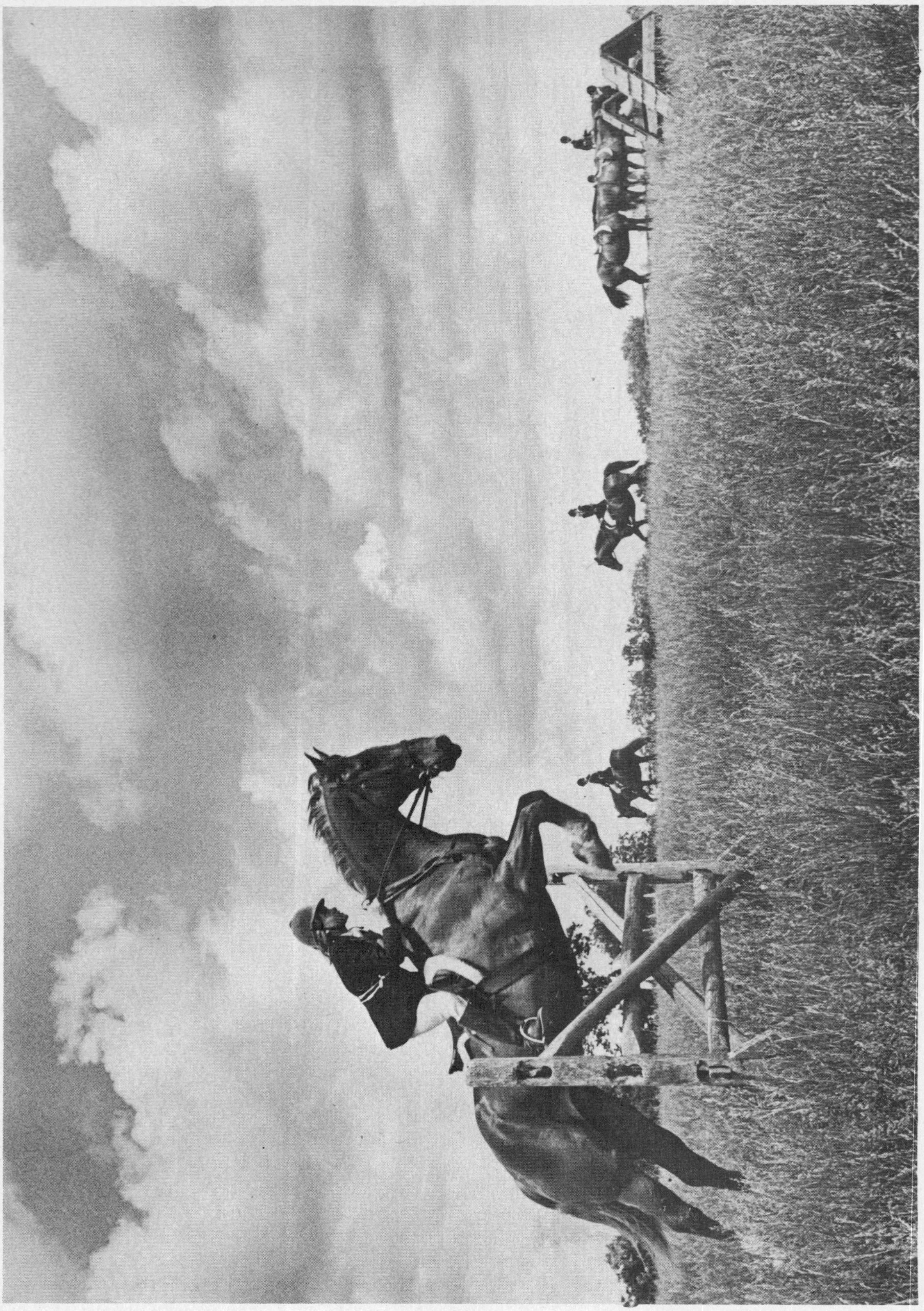

Name _____ Course _____ Date _____

_____

Crop this picture as you see fit. Then size it according to instructions provided by **your instructor**. Finally, write a cutline from the caption information provided by the photographer.

Photo Caption

Photographer
Leon Portillo

Date
Aug. 12

Department
News

Ordered by:
Enterprise

Approved:
D.L.

Caption Information
Today was a beautiful day, with a high temperature of 78 degrees, but this horse didn't have a chance to enjoy it. His owner had him locked up in his stall in a barn.

Location
Route K near Rock Bridge

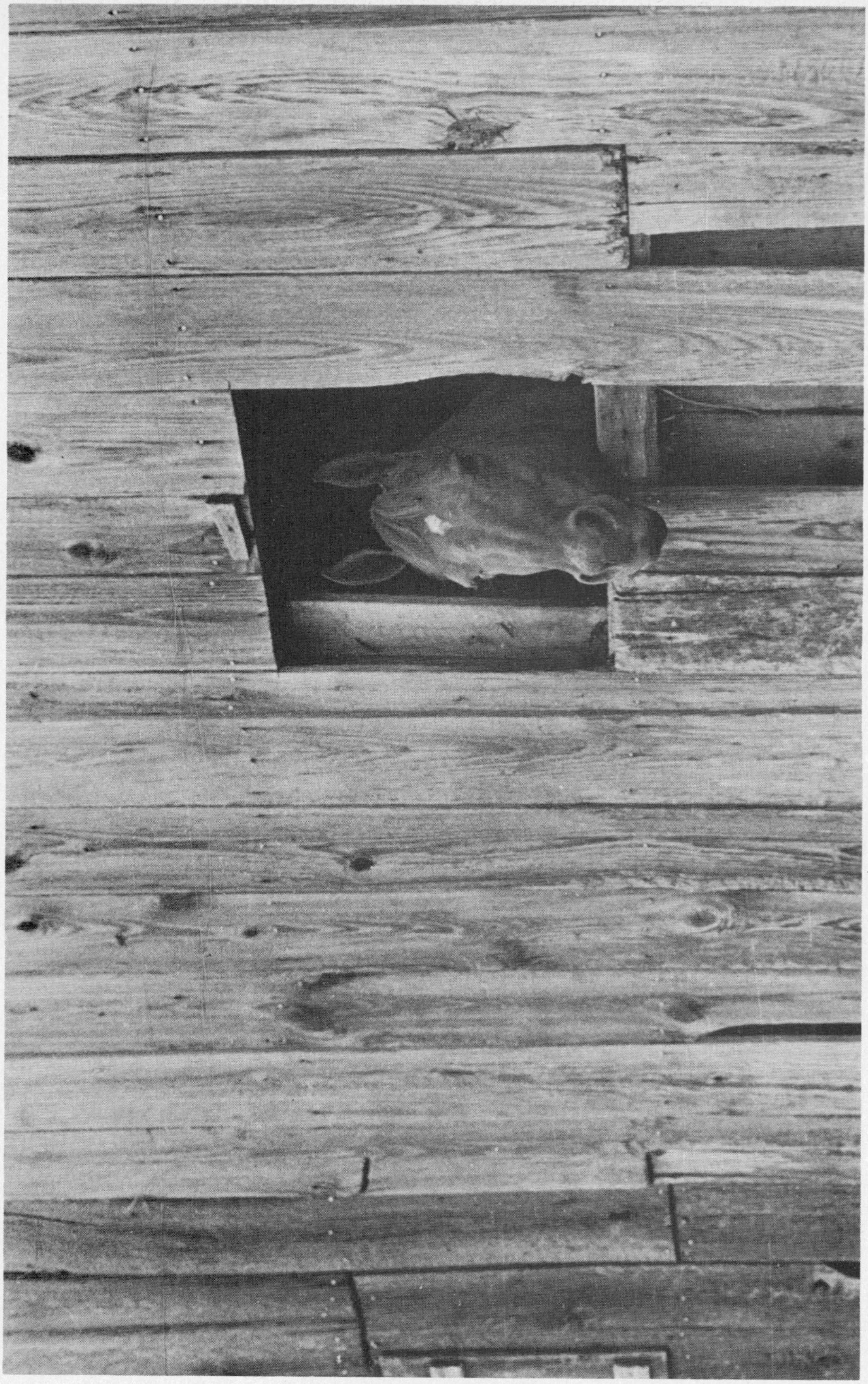

Name _____ Course _____ Date _____

_____

Crop this picture as you see fit. Then size it according to instructions provided by your instructor. Finally, write a cutline from the caption information provided by the photographer.

Photo Caption Photographer Anne Phillips Date Nov. 12 Department News Ordered by: Richardson Approved: *D.L.*	Mall Caption Information Two construction workers help put up a wall at the new City Mall being built at Stadium Blvd. and I-70 Drive S.W. The mall, which is being built by a Des Moines, Iowa, firm, will be finished next year. A department store and two discount stores will anchor the mall. Location City Mall site

—229—

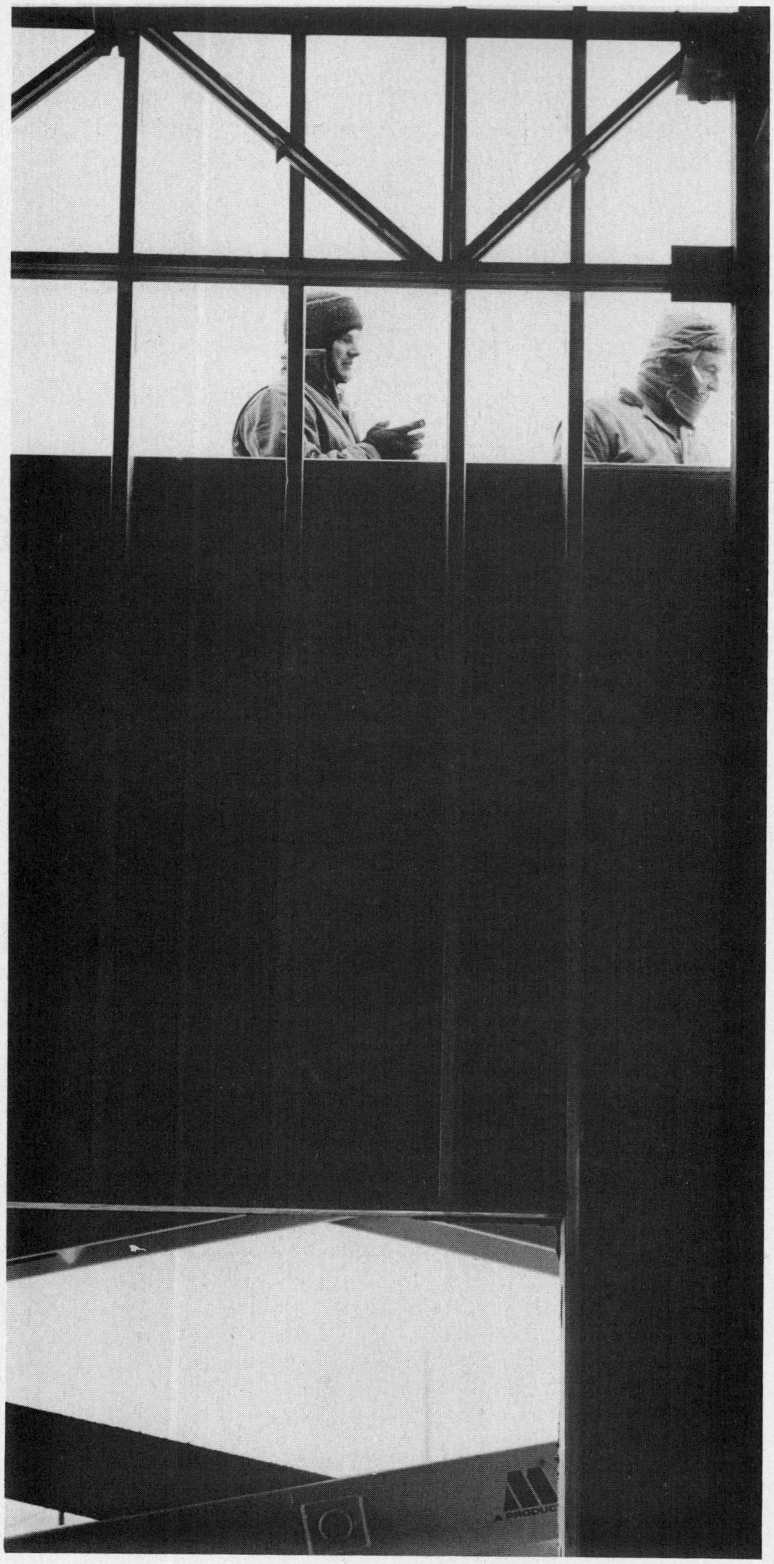

Name _____ Course _____ Date _____

_____

Crop this picture as you see fit. Then size it according to instructions provided by your instructor. Finally, write a cutline from the caption information provided by the photographer.

Photo Caption

Paint (2 pictures)

Caption Information

Dale Alexander used a new spray gun (Picture No. 1) to repaint crosswalk lines at College and Paris Road Wed. Dave helming (right) sprinkles the wet paint with finely ground glass to make the paint more visible at night. At rear is Jim Norment. They work for the State Highway Dept. At right, (picture No. 2) Ernest Roesger paints new arrows on Stadium Blvd.

Photographer
Denis Finely

Date
May 2

Department
News

Ordered by:
Todd

Approved:

Location
See above

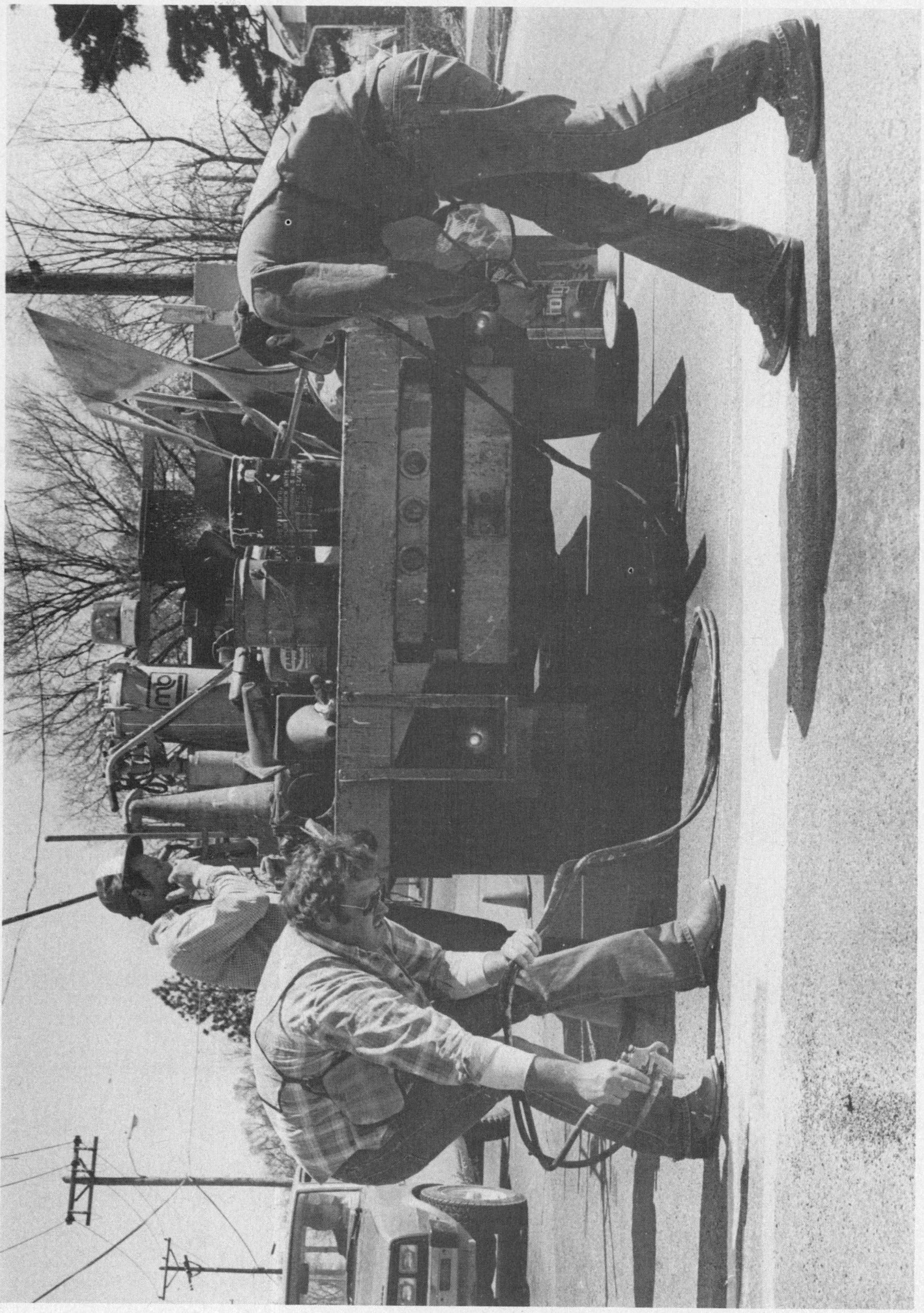

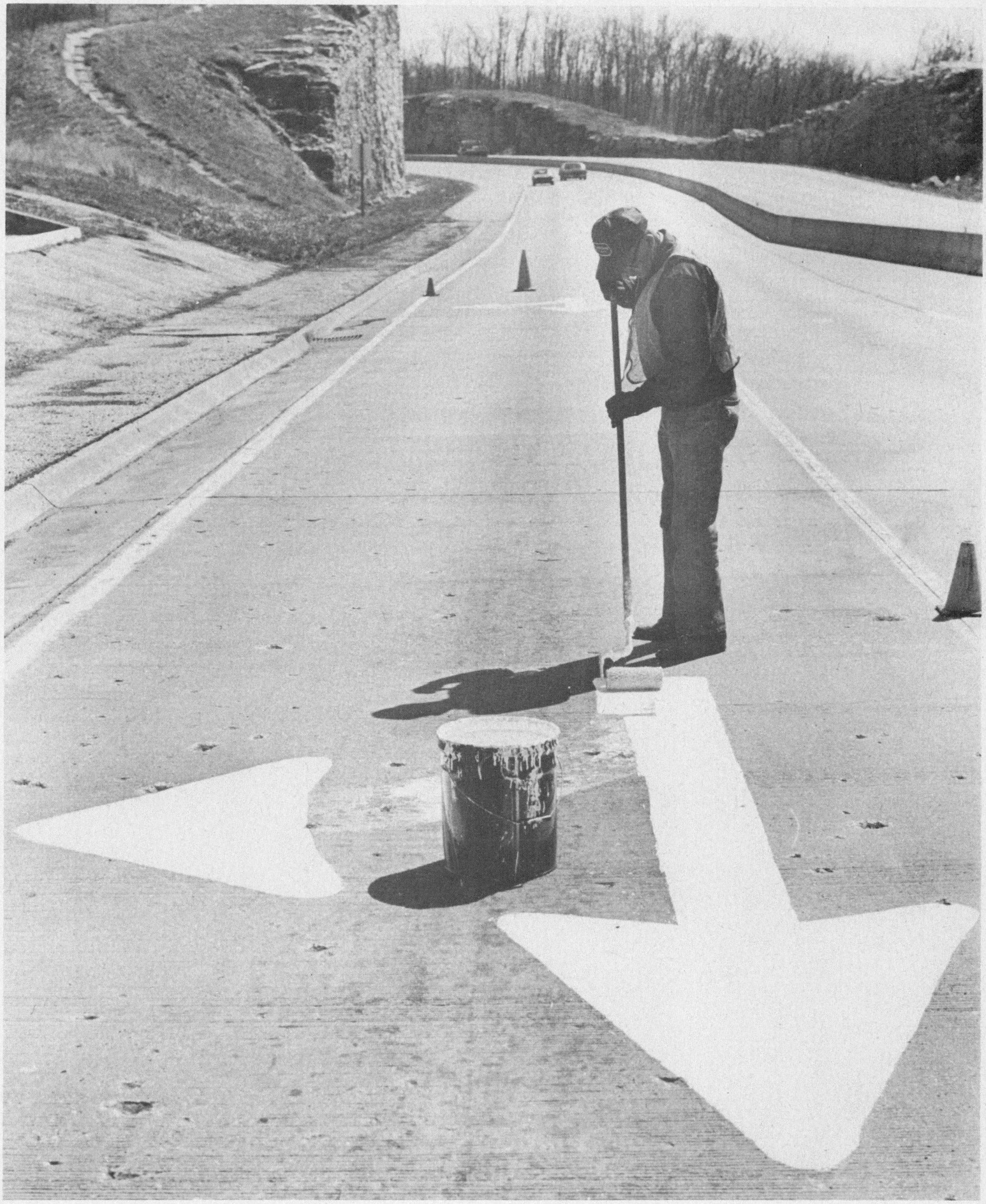

Name _____ Course _____ Date _____

Crop these pictures as you see fit. Then size them according to instructions provided by your instructor and prepare a layout for the story and pictures. Finally, write cutlines from the caption information provided by the photographer.

Photo Caption

Photographer
John Prather

Date
April 17

Department
Living

Ordered by:
Lanny Roberts

Approved:
B.K.

Caption Information
Pictures go with 8-inch article by Lanny on pasta machines and making pasta by hand. First shot shows Alice Mitchell putting dough through cutting machine. Second picture shows Grace Mitchell serving pasta. Third shows finished product on the table.

Location
Mrs. Mitchell's House, 903 E. El Cortez Dr.

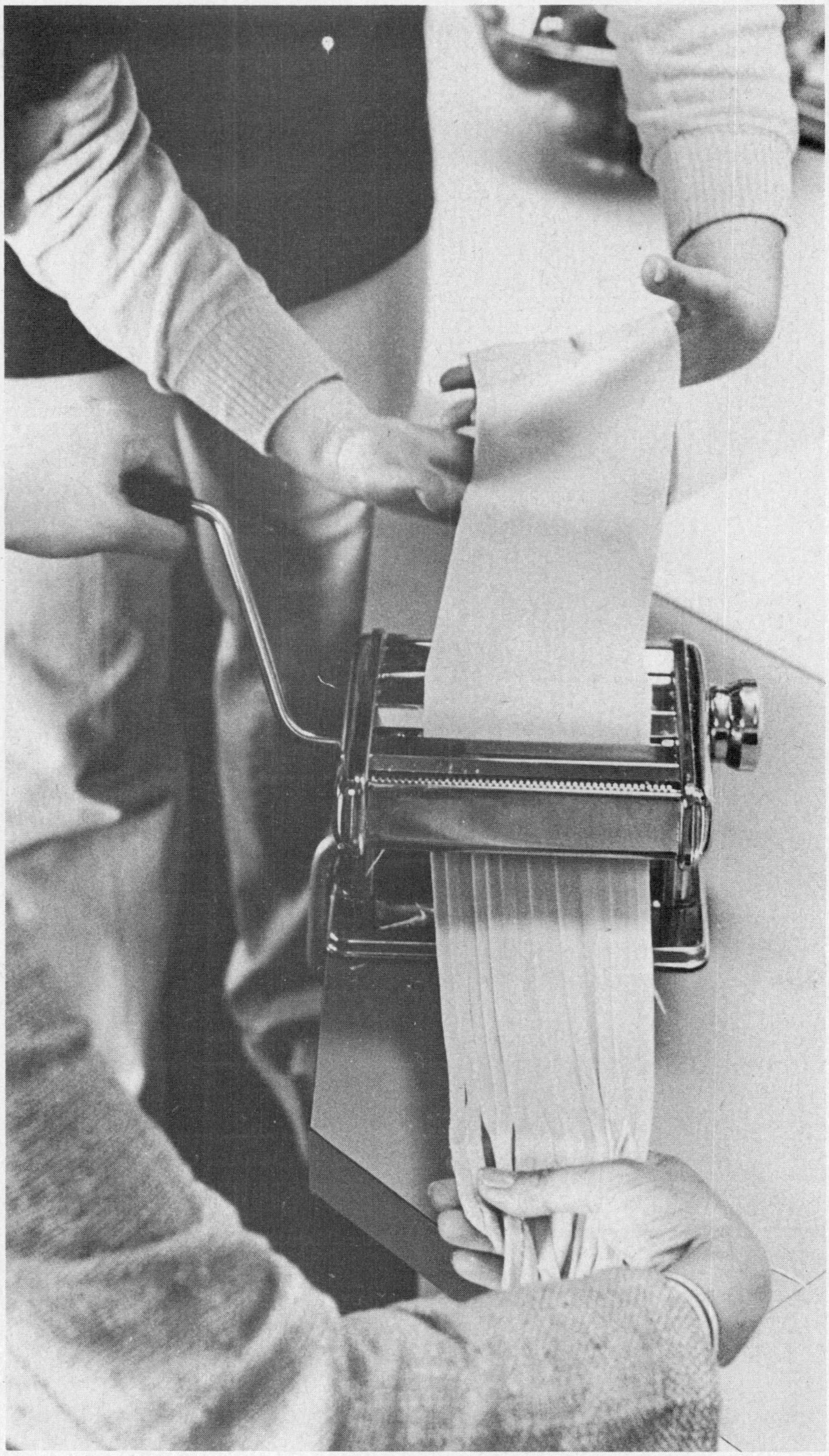

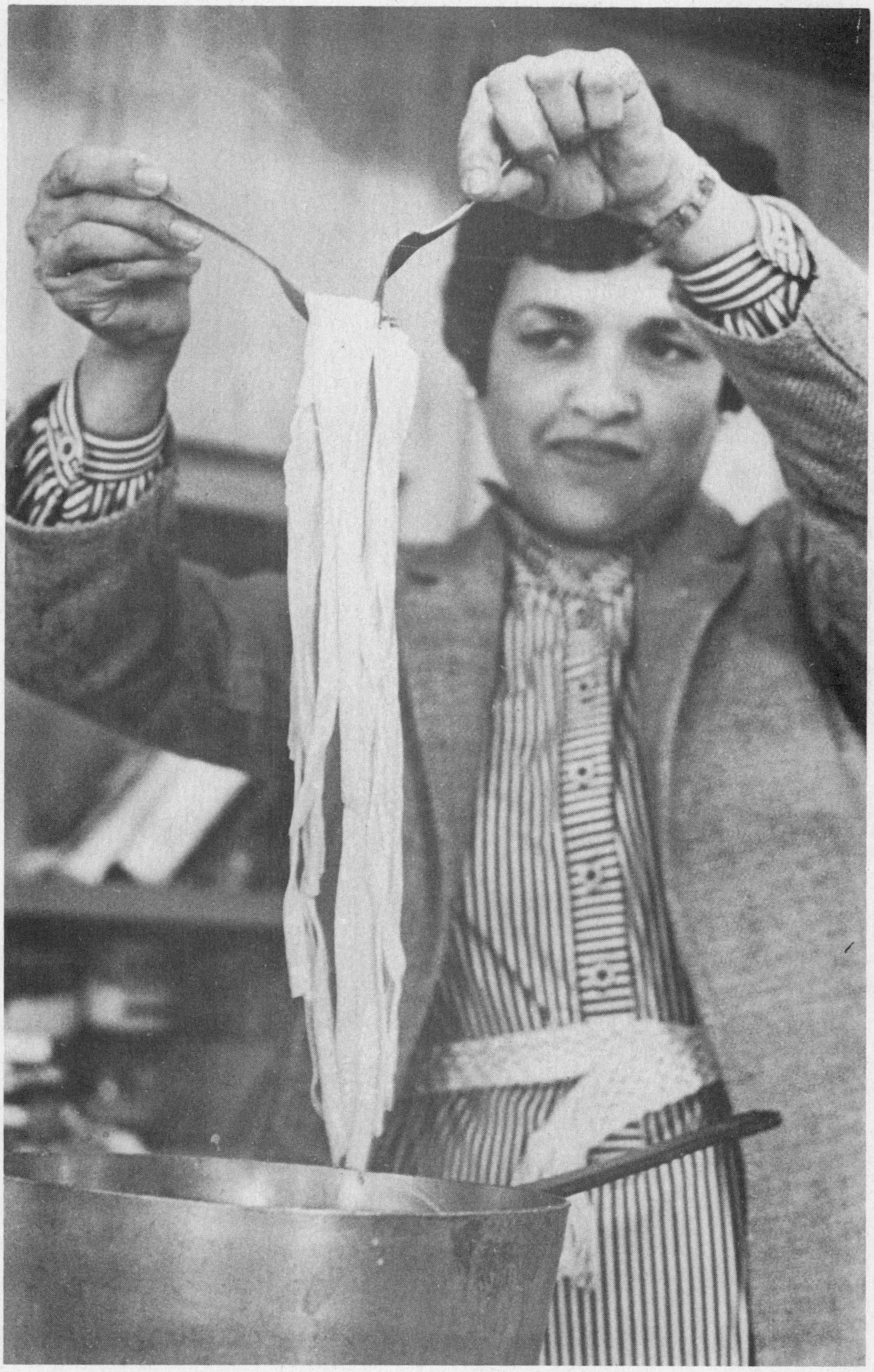

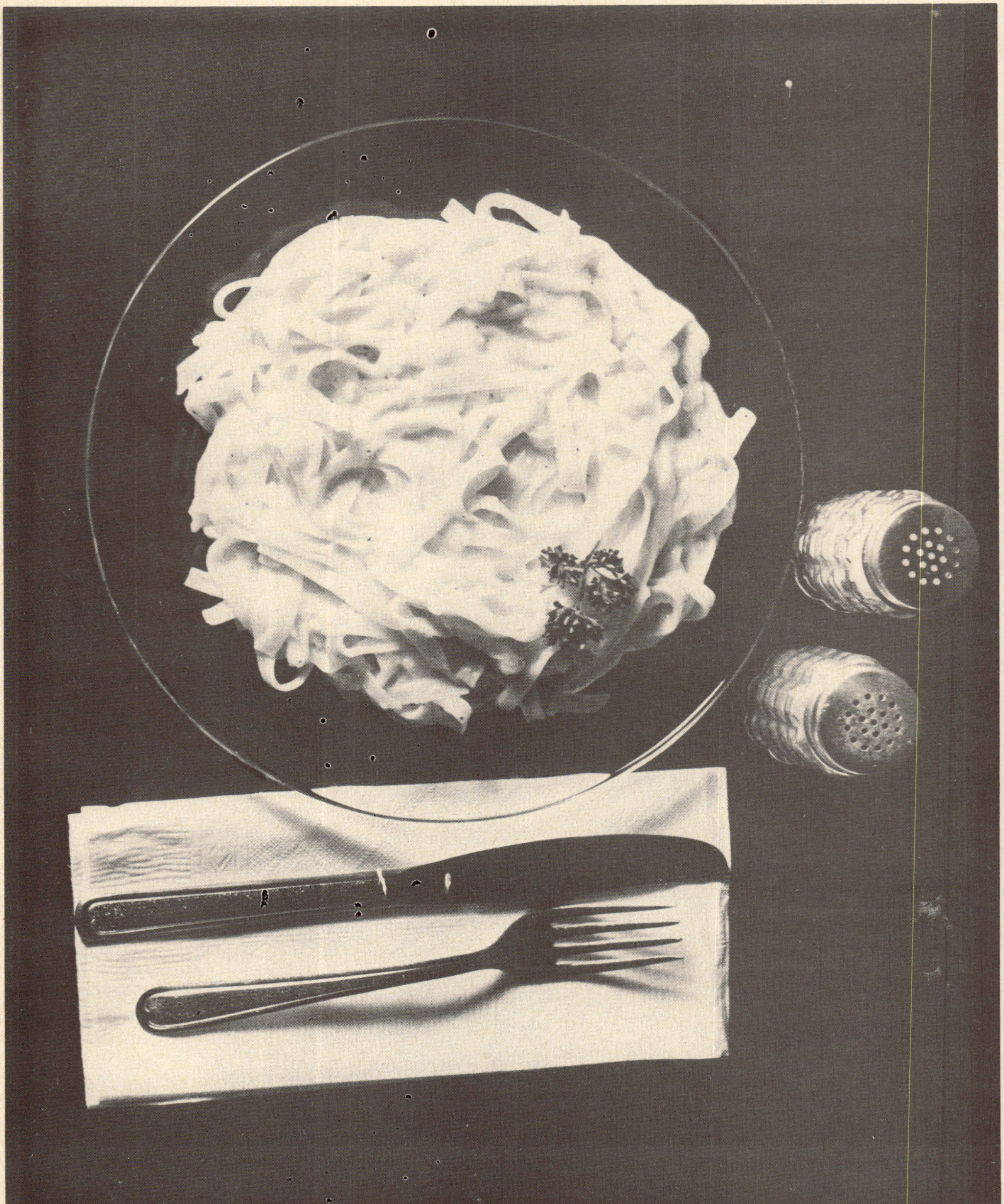

Name _____ Course _____ Date _____

Lay out an inside page using the material listed here. Your advertising dummy is on the reverse side of this page. Column width specifications may be found in Appendix V. Your instructor will tell you which stories are optional and by what amounts stories may be cut.

Editor's Copy Log

Name _____ Date _____ Desk _____

Story Slug	Time Received	Time Moved	Head Size	Length
TONER PIC	2:10	2:15	2 COL x 3½"	LINES ONLY
DOCTOR	2:20	2:45	HTK	8"
MILLER	2:25	2:50	HTK	10"
PLANK	2:30	2:55	HTK	6"

DATE_____ PAGE____ 4

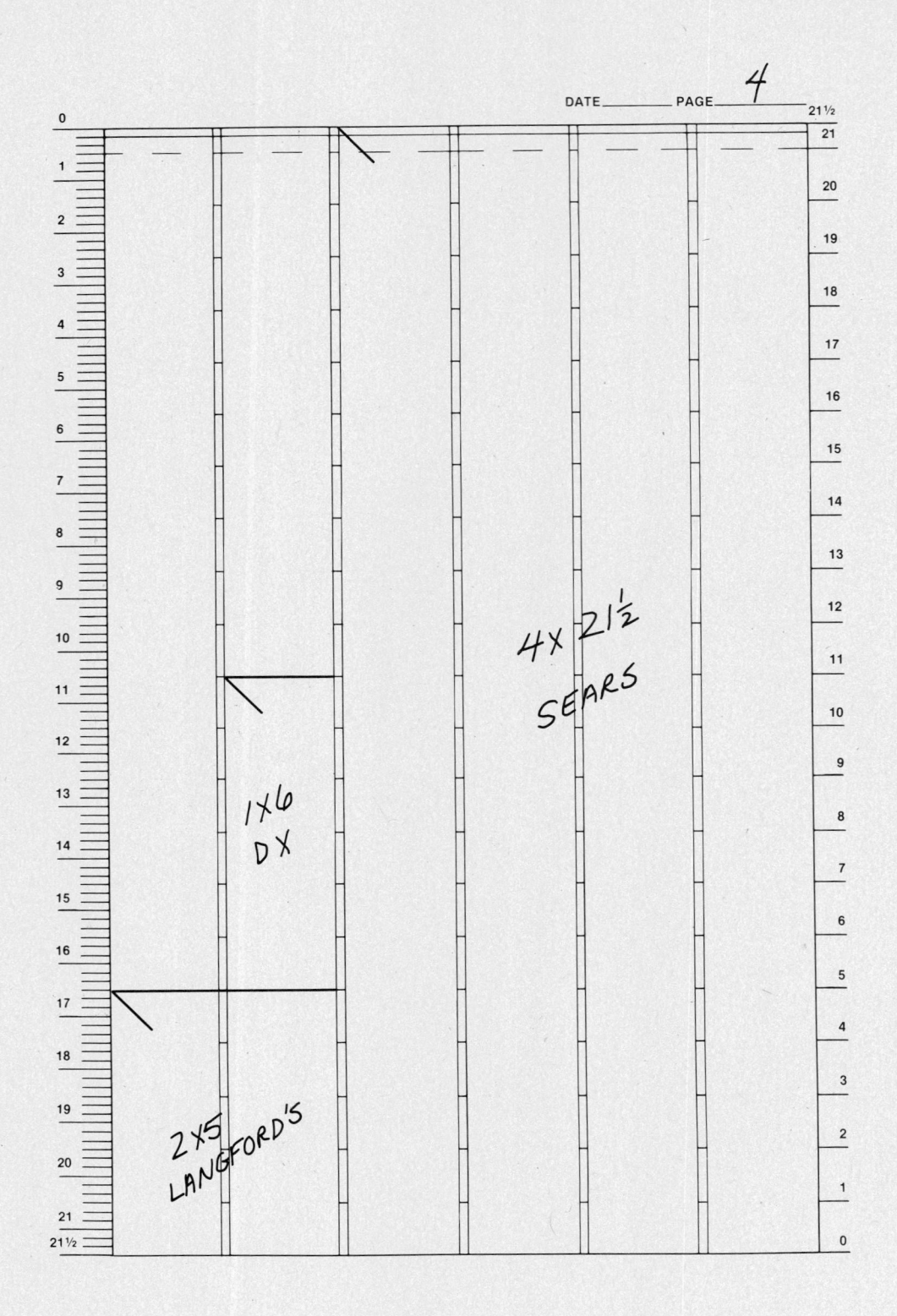

4 × 21½
SEARS

1 × 6
DX

2 × 5
LANGFORD'S

Name _____ Course _____ Date _____

Lay out an inside page using the material listed here. Your advertising dummy is on the reverse side of this page. Column width specifications may be found in Appendix V. Your instructor will tell you which stories are optional and by what amounts stories may be cut.

Editor's Copy Log

Name _____ Date _____ Desk _____

Story Slug	Time Received	Time Moved	Head Size	Length
RIDGEWAY	1:15	1:35	HTK	12"
RIDGEWAY CUT			3 COL X 6"	
MILLER	1:20	2:00	HTK	7"
LONESTAR	1:25	2:00	HTK	7½"
REINDEER	1:30	2:05	HTK	3"
FULLER	1:35	2:10	HTK	6"

DATE_____ PAGE___7___

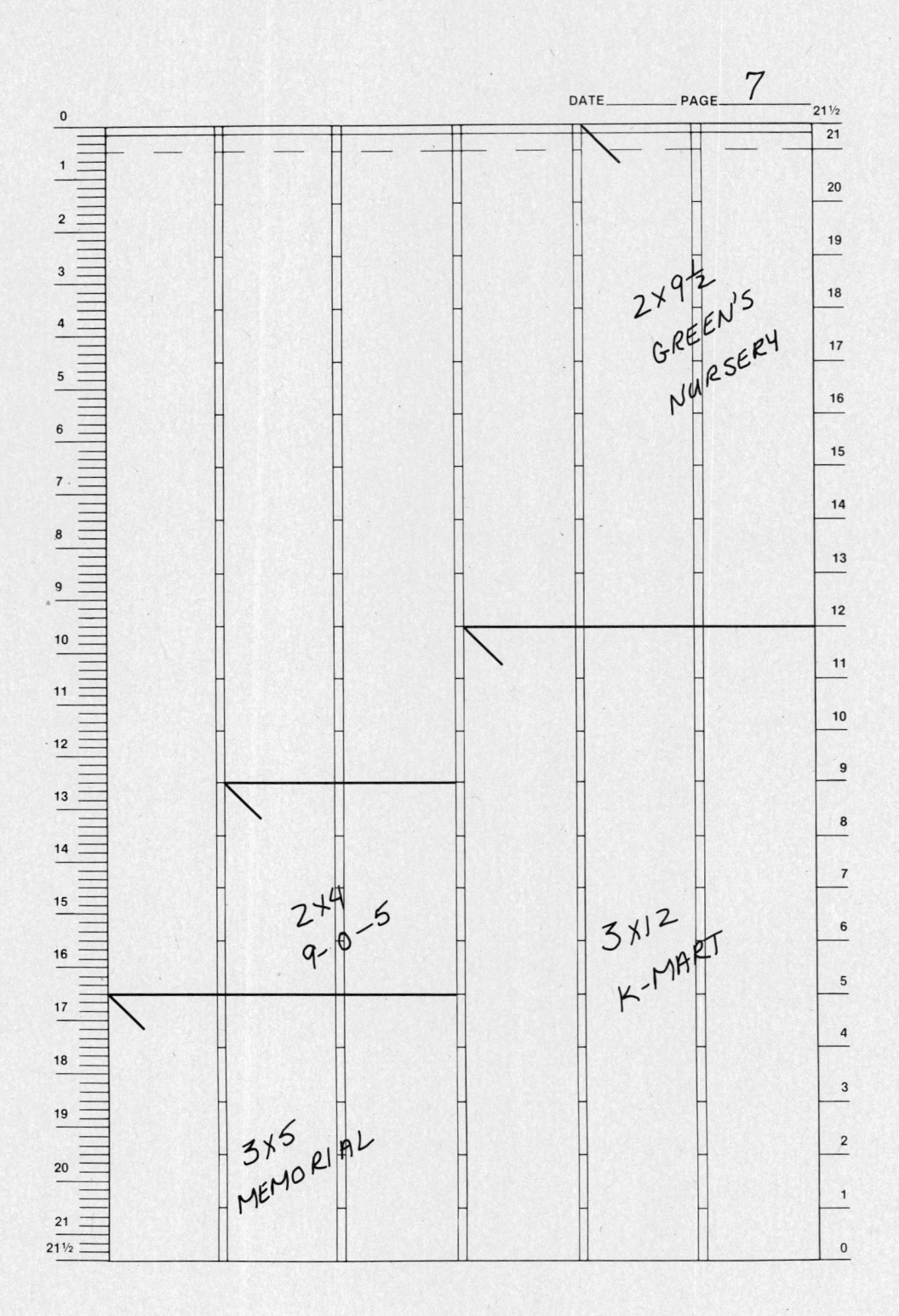

2 × 9½
GREEN'S
NURSERY

2 × 4
9-0-5

3 × 12
K-MART

3 × 5
MEMORIAL

Name _____ Course _____ Date _____

Lay out an inside page using the material listed here. Your advertising dummy is on the reverse side of this page. Column width specifications may be found in Appendix V. Your instructor will tell you which stories are optional and by what amounts stories may be cut.

Editor's Copy Log

Name _____ Date _____ Desk _____

Story Slug	Time Received	Time Moved	Head Size	Length
SCHMIDT	4:20	4:35	HTK	6"
ISRAEL	4:30	4:50	HTK	8"
ISRAEL PIC			3 COL X 4"	
LEBANON	4:35	4:50		6"
VATICAN	4:35	4:55	HTK	12"
AFRICA	4:40	5:00	HTK	8"
MEXICO	4:40	5:05	HTK	5"
ULSTER	4:45	5:05	HTK	10"
MILLER	4:45	5:00	HTK	2½"

DATE_____ PAGE__3__

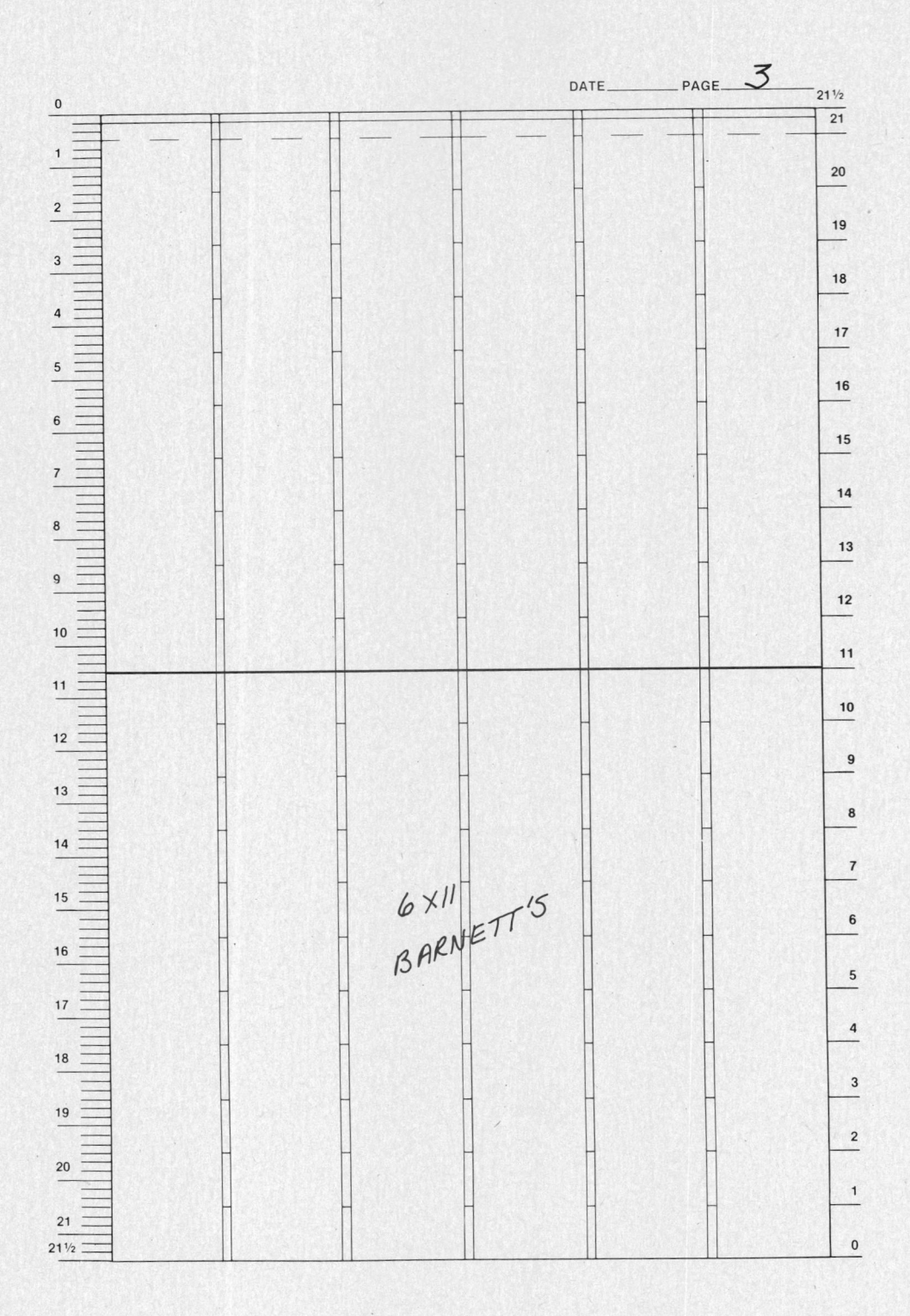

6 X 11
BARNETT'S

Name _____ Course _____ Date _____

_____

Lay out an inside page using the material listed here. Your advertising dummy is on the reverse side of this page. Column width specifications may be found in Appendix V. Your instructor will tell you which stories are optional and by what amounts stories may be cut.

Editor's Copy Log

Name _____ Date _____ Desk _____

Story Slug	Time Received	Time Moved	Head Size	Length
ATLANTA	2:05	2:30	HTK	12"
BANK	2:05	2:35	HTK	8"
MUSIC	2:08	2:40	HTK	9"
SCHOOL	2:10	2:40	HTK	8"
SCHOOL PIC			2 COL X 4"	
GRAVE	2:15	2:45		5"
DONOR	2:20	2:50	HTK	12"

DATE_____ PAGE____ 6

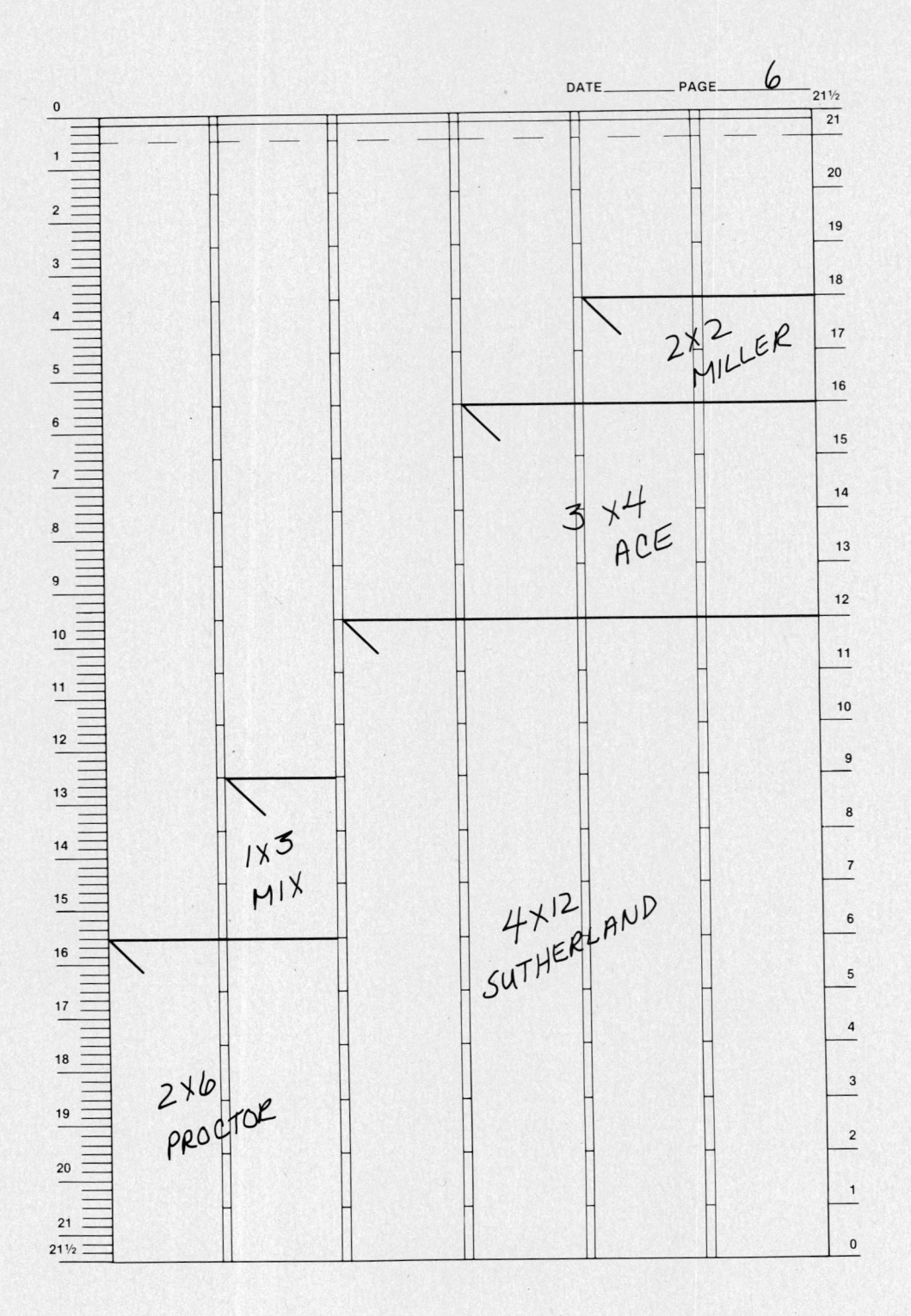

2x2 MILLER

3 x 4 ACE

1 x 3 MIX

4 x 12 SUTHERLAND

2 x 6 PROCTOR

Name _____ Course _____ Date _____

Lay out an inside page using the material listed here. Your advertising dummy is on the reverse side of this page. Column width specifications may be found in Appendix V. Your instructor will tell you which stories are optional and by what amounts stories may be cut.

Editor's Copy Log

Name _____ Date _____ Desk _____

Story Slug	Time Received	Time Moved	Head Size	Length
OVERDOSE	3:10	3:25	HTK	10"
SENATE	3:15	3:25	HTK	9"
STREIBIG	3:25	3:45	HTK	9"
STREIBIG PIC			2 COL X 5"	
DEATHS	3:25	3:45	HTK	6"
CALIFORNIA	3:30	3:50	HTK	4"

DATE_____ PAGE __2__

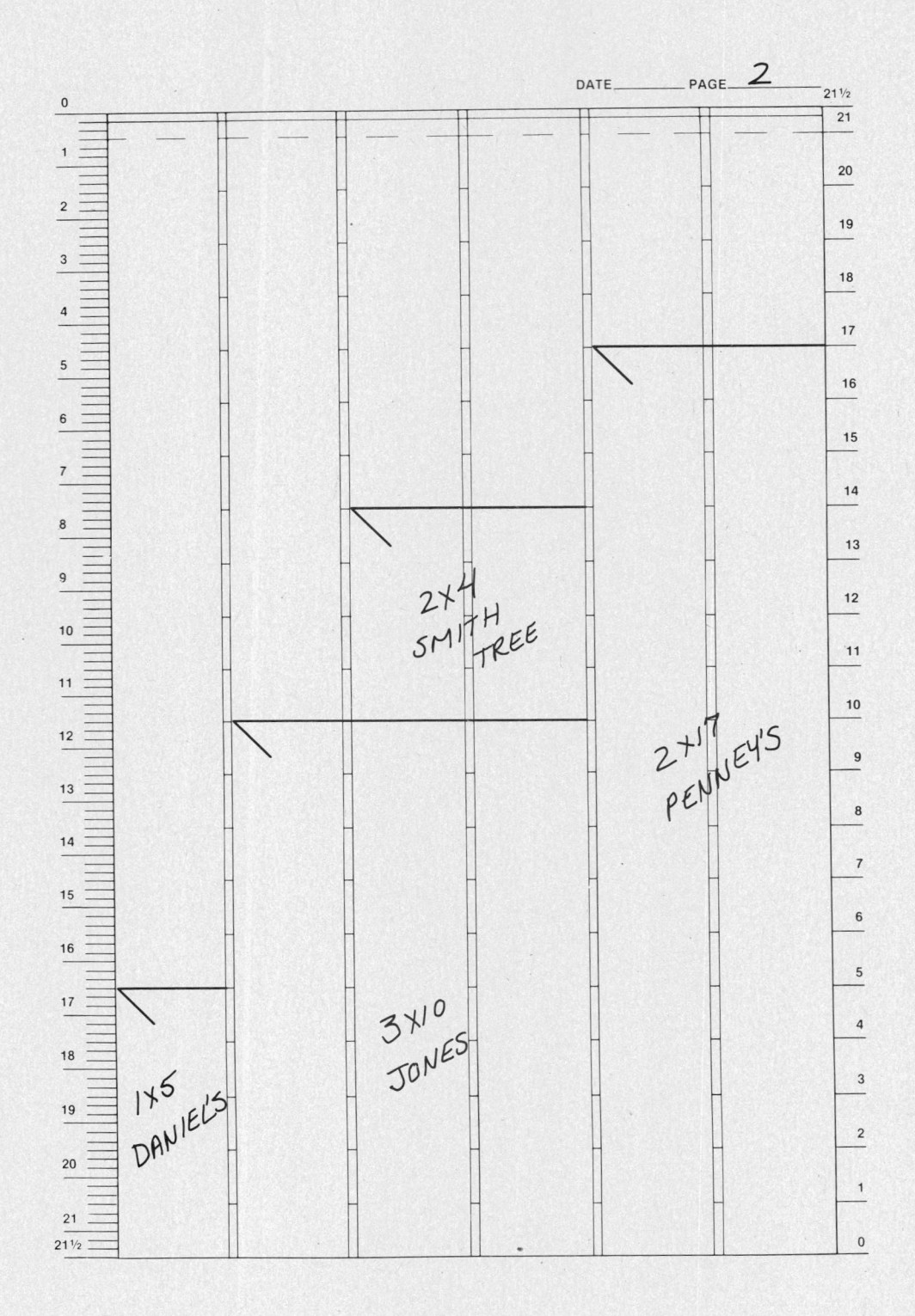

1x5
DANIEL'S

3x10
JONES

2x4
SMITH
TREE

2x17
PENNEY'S

Name _____ Course _____ Date _____

Lay out a front page using the material listed here. Your dummy is on the reverse side of this page. Column width specifications may be found in Appendix V. The flag is two inches deep. Your instructor will provide further instructions.

Editor's Copy Log

Name _____ Date _____ Desk _____

Story Slug	Time Received	Time Moved	Head Size	Length
TRAIN PIC	5:00		3 col x 5"	CUTLINE ONLY
MILLER	5:15	5:45	HTK	10"
WILTON	5:20	5:55	HTK	12"
DENTON	5:25	6:00	HTK	8"
ROUNDUP	5:30	6:10	HTK	15"
PRESIDENT	5:40	6:20	HTK	20"
AIM PIC	5:45		4 col x 5"	CUTLINE ONLY

DATE_____ PAGE_____

Name _____ Course _____ Date _____

Lay out a front page using the material listed here. Your dummy is on the reverse side of this page. Column width specifications may be found in Appendix V. The flag is two inches deep. Your instructor will provide further instructions.

Editor's Copy Log

Name _____ Date _____ Desk _____

Story Slug	Time Received	Time Moved	Head Size	Length
BUDGET	9:25	9:50	HTK	12"
BUDGET CHARTS (2)			2 COL X 4 (both)	
MAYOR	9:40	10:25	HTK	9"
MIDEAST	9:50	10:35	HTK	15"
WEATHER CUT	(lines only)		3 COL X 6"	
TRIP	10:10	10:43	HTK	12"
TRIP CUT			1 COL X 3"	
SENATE	10:20	11:00	HTK	9"
THINK	10:25	11:10	HTK	6"

DATE_____ PAGE_____

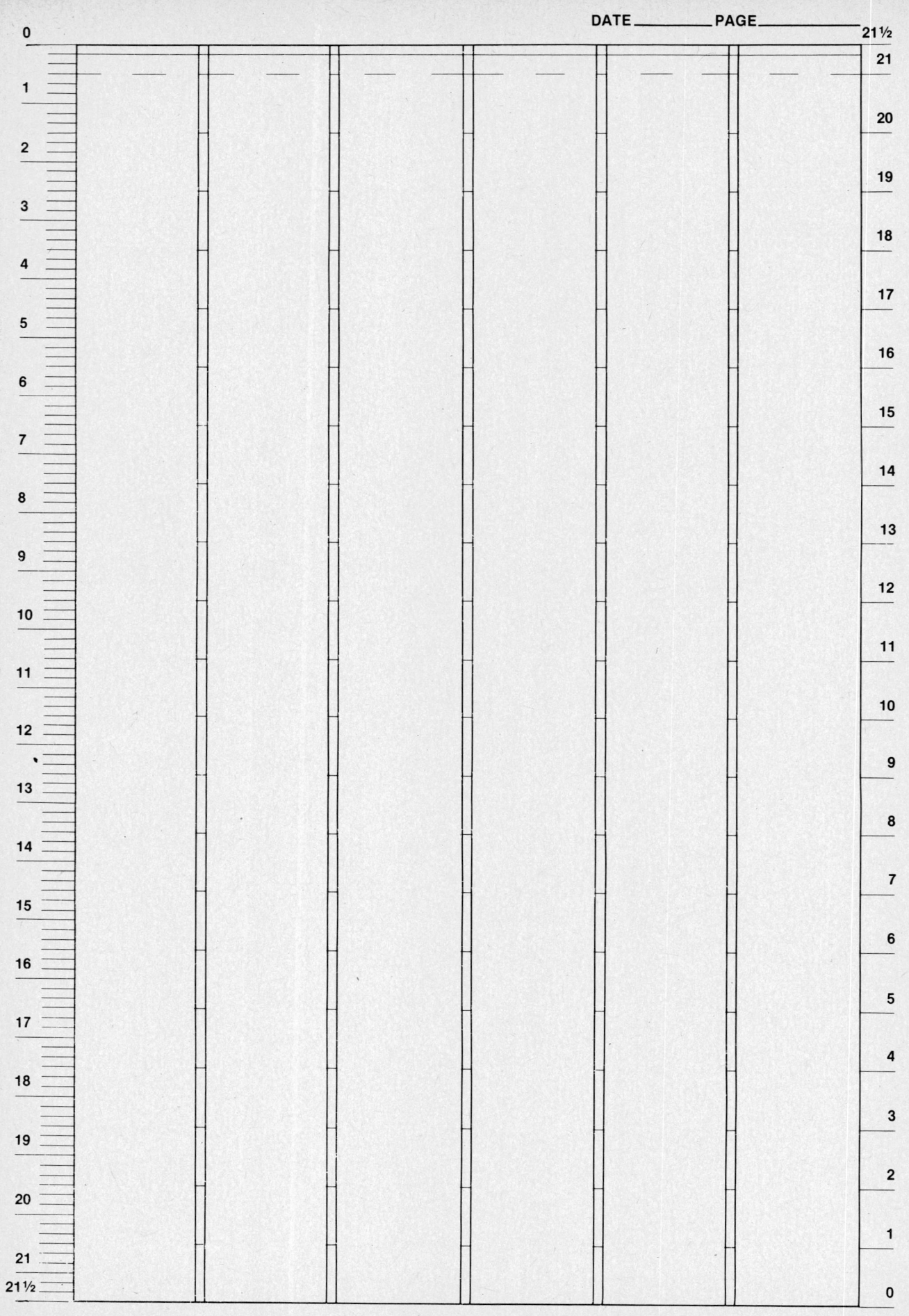

Name _____ Course _____ Date _____

Lay out a front page using the material listed here. Your dummy is on the reverse side of this page. Column width specifications may be found in Appendix V. The flag is two inches deep. Your instructor will provide further instructions.

Editor's Copy Log

Name _____ Date _____ Desk _____

Story Slug	Time Received	Time Moved	Head Size	Length
MIDEAST	9:00	9:25	HTK	22"
MIDEAST CUT			4 COL x 5"	
PRESIDENT	9:15	9:45	HTK	12"
SOCIAL	9:25	10:05	HTK	10"
INSIGHT	10:15	10:35	HTK	20"
TRAIN	10:55	11:40	HTK	10"
TRAIN MAP			1 COL x 4"	
LEND	11:10	11:45	HTK	6"

DATE_____ PAGE_____

Name _____ Course _____ Date _____

Lay out a front page using the material listed here. Your dummy is on the reverse side of this page. Column width specifications may be found in Appendix V. The flag is two inches deep. Your instructor will provide further instructions.

Editor's Copy Log

Name _____ Date _____ Desk _____

Story Slug	Time Received	Time Moved	Head Size	Length
FISH CUT	(lines only)		4 col x 5"	
PRESIDENT	9:45	10:20	HTK	20"
LEAP	10:00	10:30	HTK	10"
LEADER	10:05	10:30	HTK	6"
LEADER CUT			1 col x 3"	
CIRCUS	10:15	10:45	HTK	8"
ROB	10:25	11:15	HTK	14"
FOCUS	10:35	11:20	HTK	6"

DATE ________ PAGE ________

0 1 2 3 4 5 6 7 8 9 10 11 12 13 14 15 16 17 18 19 20 21 21½

21½ 21 20 19 18 17 16 15 14 13 12 11 10 9 8 7 6 5 4 3 2 1 0

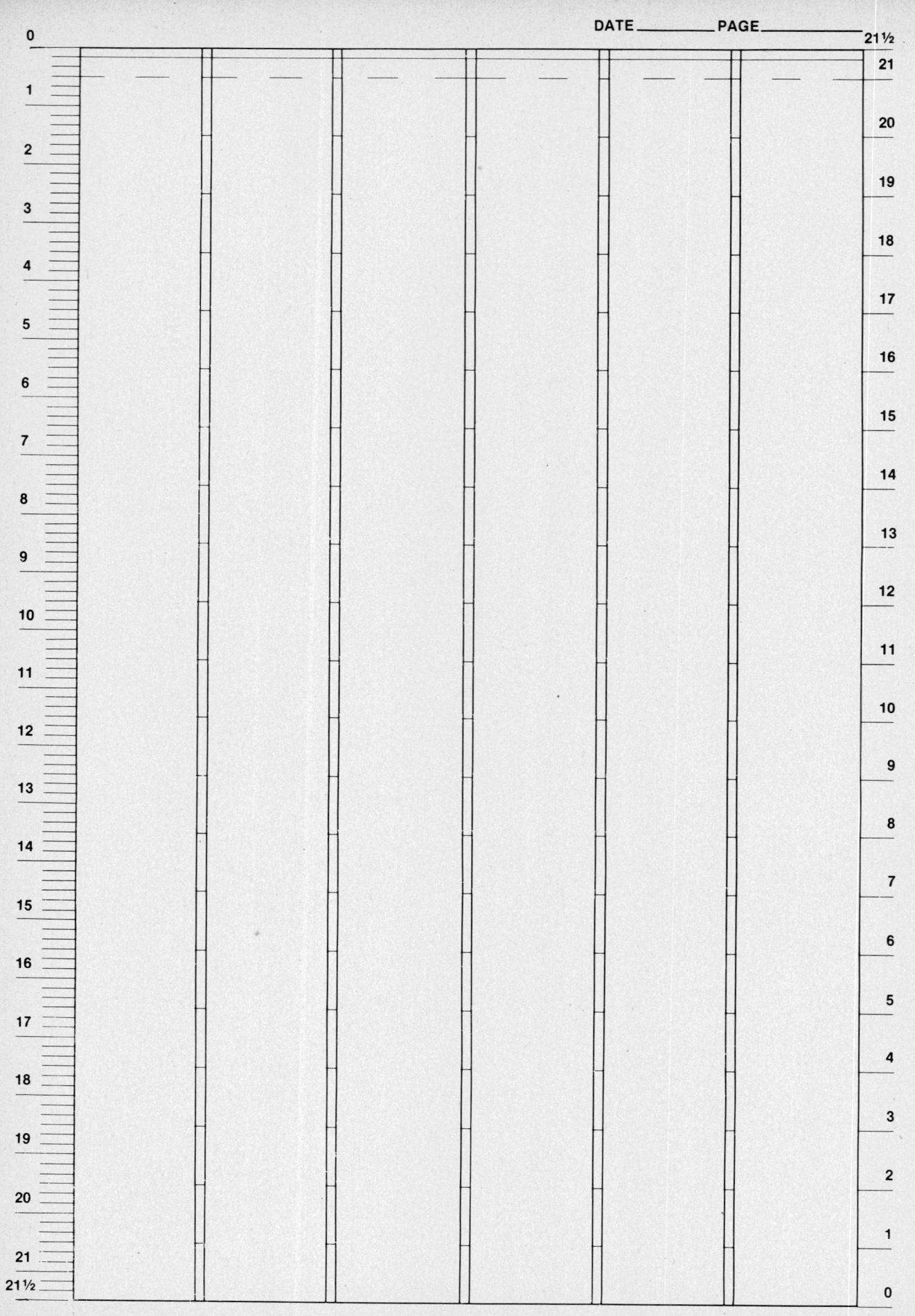

Name _____ Course _____ Date _____

Lay out a front page using the material listed here. Your dummy is on the reverse side of this page. Column width specifications may be found in Appendix V. The flag is two inches deep. Your instructor will provide further instructions.

Editor's Copy Log

Name _____ Date _____ Desk _____

Story Slug	Time Received	Time Moved	Head Size	Length
IRELAND	9:30	9:55	HTK	14"
IRELAND CUTS	(2) 3 COL	X 4½" &	1 COL X 3"	
BLAST	10:20	11:00	HTK	12"
CENTER	11:00	11:25	HTK	6"
DRANE CUT	(W/CENTER)		1 COL X 3"	
TORNADO	11:25	11:45	HTK	10"
MAYOR	11:25	11:50	HTK	9"
WILSON	11:30	11:50	HTK	6"

DATE_____ PAGE_____

SECTION V

EDITING FOR OTHER MEDIA

Problems

MAGAZINE EDITING

1. In what ways does magazine editing differ from newspaper editing?

2. Determine the imposition pattern for a 24-page magazine.

BROADCAST NEWS EDITING

1. In what ways does newspaper editing differ from radio news editing? In what ways does newspaper editing differ from television news editing?

2. Television's greatest asset is immediacy. If a story of a major flood in your city receives lengthy coverage on television, what can you, as a newspaper editor, do to supplement that coverage hours later?

SECTION VI

A LOOK TO THE FUTURE

Problems

NEWSPAPERS AND THE FUTURE

1. Research at your local library the current status of home information retrieval systems in this country. Tell whether you think such systems pose a threat to newspapers. Support your opinions with reasoned judgments.

2. It is the year 2010 and you are the editor of one of the nation's few remaining independent metro dailies. The nation's largest newspaper chain has asked you to testify before the U.S. Senate in support of a bill that would provide tax breaks for newspapers in the face of increasing competition from home retrieval systems. Will you testify? Why or why not?

APPENDIX I

SYMBOLS

Copy Editing

Indent for new paragraph

(no ¶) No paragraph (in margin)

Run in or bring copy together

Join words: week end

Insert a *single* word or phrase

Insert a missing letter

Take out ant extra letter

Transpose words two

Transpose tow letters

Make Letter lower case

Capitalize columbia

Indicate *italic* letters

Indicate small capitals

Indicate bold face type

Abbreviate (January) 30

Spell out (abbrev.)

Spell out number (9)

Make figures of (thirteen)

Separate run together words

Join letters in a w ord

Insert period ⊙

Insert comma ⋀

Insert quotation marks ⌄⌄ ⌄⌄

Take out ~~some~~ word

Don't make ~~this~~ correction (STET)

Mark] centering [like this

] Indent copy from both sides [by using these marks

] Indent copy on left

Spell name Smyth as written

or

Spell name Smyth as written (f.c.)

There's more story: (MORE)

This ends story: # (30)

Do not obliterate copy; mark it out ~~with a thin line~~ so it can be compared with editing.

Mark in hyphen: =

Mark in dash: ⊢⊣

a̲ and u̲

ō and n̄

Proofreading

∧	Insert at this point.	✓✓	Space evenly.
⊥	Push down space.	⌒	Close up entirely.
ℓ	Take out letter, letters, or words.	⊏	Move to left.
ꙅ	Turn inverted letter.	⊐	Move to right.
(lc)	Set lowercase.	⊔	Lower letter or word.
(wf)	Wrong font letter.	⊓	Raise letter or word.
(ital)	Reset in italic type.	(out, see copy)	Words are left out.
(rom)	Reset in roman (regular) type.	∥ ═	Straighten lines.
(bf)	Reset in bold face type.	(¶)	Start new paragraph.
⊙	Insert period.	(no ¶)	No paragraph. Run together.
⌃	Insert comma.	(tr)	Transpose letters or words.
⌃	Insert semicolon.	(?)	Query; is copy right?
H	Insert hyphen.	⊢⊣	Insert dash.
⌵	Insert apostrophe.	□	Indent 1 em.
⌵⌵	Enclose in quotation marks.	□□	Indent 2 ems.
≡	Replace with a capital letter.	□□□	Indent 3 ems.
#	Insert space.	(stet)	Let it stand.

APPENDIX II

HEADLINE SCHEDULE

This headline schedule lists the unit count (maximum count) per line of headlines of the indicated column width and type size. It does not list each headline by number of lines since, for example, the count per line for a 1-24-2 would be the same as that for a 1-24-3.

ENGLISH BOLD

Headline	Maximum	Headline	Maximum	Headline	Maximum
1-14	21	4-36	39	4-60	23 1/2
1-18	18	1-48	6 1/2	5-60	30
1-24	13	2-48	14	6-60	36
2-24	26 1/2	3-48	21	2-72	7
1-30	10 1/2	4-48	29	3-72	14 1/2
2-30	23	5-48	37	4-72	20
1-36	9	6-48	44	5-72	24 1/2
2-36	19	2-60	11 1/2	6-72	30
3-36	29	3-60	17 1/2		

Avoid using headlines not listed above. For example, 14English would not be used across two columns.

ENGLISH LIGHT

Headline	Maximum	Headline	Maximum	Headline	Maximum
1-14	22	4-36	42	4-60	25 1/2
1-18	19	1-48	7	5-60	32
1-24	14	2-48	15	6-60	38 1/2
2-24	29	3-48	23 1/2	2-72	7 1/2
1-30	11	4-48	31 1/2	3-72	15 1/2
2-30	24	5-48	40	4-72	21 1/2
1-36	9 1/2	6-48	48	5-72	26 1/2
2-36	20 1/2	2-60	12 1/2	6-72	32
3-36	31	3-60	19		

ENGLISH EXTRABOLD

Headline	Maximum	Headline	Maximum	Headline	Maximum
1-14	16	1-30	8	1-60	4
1-18	13	1-36	6 1/2	1-72	3
1-24	10 1/2	1-48	5		

Note: To figure the maximum count for English Extrabold headlines of more than one column, multiply the maximum for one column by the number of columns.

APPENDIX III

CITY DIRECTORY

—A—

A&B Maintenance Management Co.,
 512 Cherry St.
A—1 Insulation,
 730 W. Sexton Rd.
Alderson, Robert M. & Wanda (gen mgr, Boone
 Electric Co-op), Route 5
Altomani, Mark & Diana (director, Associates in
 Human Services), 209 Lynnwood Dr.
Aly, Thomas (emp unk),
 2369 Ridge Rd.
Ambaugh, Mrs. Ardath (retired),
 Senior Citizens Center
American Red Cross,
 1805 W. Worley St.
Amundson, Erik K. (student),
 2012 W. Ash St., Apt. D5
Anderson, David & Lena M (retired),
 913 N. Garth Ave.
Apon, Ruth N. (sr. stenographer, University),
 110 N. Glenwood Ave.
Ash, Kenneth (University Health Sciences Ctr),
 312 Sanford Ave.

—B—

Barnes Pat & Mimi (asst chief, Boone County
 Fire Prot. Dist.), 4202 W. Rollins Rd.
Bashor, Terry W. & Diane E. (asst. dean, University),
 1317 Overhill Rd.
Beck, Raymond A. & Delilah (dir, city public works),
 201 Sappington Dr.
Bell, Dennis (mgr, University),
 Rt. 1 Hallsville
Belvedere Apartments,
 206 Hitt St.
Birmingham, Dan (Associates in Human Services),
 2002 Hinkson Ave.
Black, Robert D. & Jean C (asst city mgr),
 812 Maupin Rd.
Blackwell, Doris C. (asst to pres, First Bank of
 Commerce), Rt. 2
Board of Education,
 1818 W. Worley St.
Boone County Bank,
 720 E. Broadway
Boone Electric Co-operative,
 1413 Business 63 N.
Borman, Debra (emp unk),
 1901 E. Walnut St., Apt. 3
Boston, Diane (housekeeper, VA Hospital),
 9 Business 63 S., Apt. 16
Bowman, Kevin (Boone County Glass),
 2901 Greenbriar Dr.
Bradford, Betty (janitor),
 800 Wilkes Blvd.
Brill, Patricia (information specialist, Boone Hospital
 Ctr), 2145 Auburn Lane.

Brown, Nate (newspaper executive),
 210 Stalcup St.
Brydon, Earl C (laborer, Walter Strange Constr),
 734 Demaret Dr.
Bulgin Development Co.,
 301 Vieux Carre Ct.
Bulgin, Lawrence & Jackie, (owner, Bulgin
 Development Co.), 810 E. Taylor St.
Burger King,
 2015 W. Broadway
Burnette, Ray W. & Margaret A (constr worker,
 John Epple Constr Co), 208 St. Joseph St.

—C—

Calvary Baptist Church,
 606 Ridgeway Ave.
Campbell, Charles C. & Penny A. (assoc provost,
 University), 811 Sycamore Lane
Carnes, Lloyd E (retired),
 709 W. Sexton Rd.
Cave, John (circuit ct judge),
 Route 8
Central Bridge Co.,
 Stadium Blvd. at West Broadway
Christ-Janer, Arland F. & Sally (pres, Stephens Coll),
 3400 Woodrail Terr, Apt. 1
Coca-Cola Bottling Co,
 1601 Business 63 S.
Commerce Bank,
 500 Business Loop 70 W.
Community Rehabilitation Center,
 1101 Hinkson Ave.
Cowznofsky, Melvin (supt, Midway Hts School Dist),
 Route 3
Crawford, George E. & Jennie (pres, Crawford Const
 Co.), 2220 Shepard Blvd.
Crawford, George W. & Pearl L. (retired),
 510 W. Worley St.
Cullen, Barbara (sls associate, Action Realty),
 1805A Stanford

—D—

D Sport Shop,
 1034 E. Walnut St.
Daniel Boone Regional Library,
 100 W. Broadway
Davis, Peter N. & Mary L (prof, University),
 700 S. Greenwood Ave.
Dennison, David (student),
 2712A Quail Dr.
Dersham, Watson W. & Rosalie W. (dir, Amer Heart
 Assn), 604 W. Texas Ave.
Diekmann, John H. & Marilyn M. (asst mgr, Safeway),
 2605 Andy Dr.
Diver's Village,
 131 S. 7th St.

Doak, David (asst public def),
    303 West Blvd. N.
Doelger, Mary J (collection clrk, Orthopedic Grp),
    2305 Meadowlark Lane
Downs, Cathy J (student),
    2401 W. Broadway, Apt. 119
Downtown Appliance Co., 1104 E. Broadway
Drexler, James S. & Vita A (University extension),
    2901 Burrwood Dr.
Dueblar, Jan (vocational evaluator),
    105 Albany, Apt. D

—E—

Easley, Blanche H. Mrs. (retired),
    913 Sandifer Ave.
Ellis Fischel State Cancer Hospital,
    115 Business Loop 70 W.
Elmore, Stuart (manager, North County grocery),
    537 Benton St.
Enyart, Carl & Yolanda (tech, 3-M Co.),
    3500 Vista Place
Estep, Glenda (secretary),
    1005 N. Eighth St.
Estes, Jack & Wendy (mgr, Property Sales Inc.),
    210 Sondra Ave.
Eye Care Associates,
    909 University Ave.

—F—

Fahy, Dennis (student),
    9 Business 63 S., Apt. 6
Fain, Daniel & Alida (mgr, Asphlund Tree Co.),
    3718 Southridge Dr.
Fenton, Roy H. & Minerva S. (retired),
    418 Sanford Ave.
Forrester, Gene A. & Helen (pharmacist),
    3390 Country Hill Ct.
Forsberg, Clarence J. Rev. & Ruby (United Methodist Church), 3702 Woodrail on the Green
Foster, Charles E. (sheriff),
    Route 6
First National Bank & Trust Co.,
    801 E. Broadway
First Bank of Commerce,
    8th and Cherry Streets
First Bank of Commerce East,
    5 Business 63 S.
Frech, William M. (pres judge, county court),
    Route 6
Fullington, A. & Juanita (repairman, Henderson Implement), 2704 Blue Ridge Rd.

—G—

G&D Steak House,
    2001 W. Worley St.
Garner, Patsy (pres, Bd. of Educ.),
    Route 5
Gensicke, Mavis (emp, University),
    1206 Haven Rd.
Gentry, James K. & Mary Beth (instr, University),
    1602 University Ave.
Gibbens, Chas G. & Jean (Credit Bureau),
    3300 Westcreek Dr.
Gilliam, Arthur & Naomi (baker, Stephens College),
    2708 Northridge Dr.
Glatz, Annette M. (sr acct clrk, University),
    2212 Sunflower
Gray, Richard (city manager),
    2020 Oak Haven Dr.
Gunter, Caryn M. (dir, Rape Crisis Ctr),
    2004 W. Broadway, Apt. A
Gutreuter, Mary E. (lab technician),
    Route 2

—H—

Hagemann, Virginia P. (assoc prof, University),
    1109 W. Steward Rd.
Hamory, Bruce H. (asst prof, University),
    Route 1
Harris, Hugh S. Jr. and Nancy (medical doctor),
    654 Canyon Dr.
Hartman, Gerald W. (realtor),
    2100 W. Broadway
Hazard, I.R. & Edna M. (retired),
    501 Hulen Dr.
Heniz, Cynthia E. (nurse),
    1707 McAlester
Highbarger, Carroll W. (detective, Police Department), 310 Elm St.
Hinten, John & Sharon (emp Richards Assoc.),
    2012 W. Ash St., Apt. 117
Hoffmaster, David (emp Stephens College),
    21 N. Greenwood Ave.
Holt, J.O. (retired),
    801 N. 8th St.
Hosmer, Craig (student),
    303 Waugh St.
Hubbard, Clarry & Carolyn (students),
    1614 Amelia St., Apt. 4B
Hughes, Ann (teacher),
    1100 Mehl Rd., Apt. 1A
Hultz, Tamara (student),
    2303 Whitegate Dr., Apt 3E

—I—

Installers Unlimited,
    922 Business Loop 70 E.
Interstate 70 Shell,
    1004 Stadium Blvd.
Interstate Pancake House,
    1110 I-70 Dr. S.W.

—J—

Jaeger, Roger D. & Marie A. (pres, House of Zenith),
 1101 Hulen Dr.
Jeanne's Beauty Salon,
 8 N. 2nd St.
Jeney, Agnes (cashier),
 252 W. Brookside Lane
Jennings, Bill & Colleen M. (emp, Public Schools),
 708 W. Texas Ave.
Johnson, Anne E. (technician),
 8638 Argyle
Johnson, Walter (professor),
 503 Edgewood Ave.
Johnston Audio Inc.,
 702 E. Broadway
Jones, Edward D. & Co.,
 907 E. Broadway
Jorgenson, Charles M. (artist),
 15 Quaker Circle

—K—

KBIA Radio,
 310 Jesse Hall, University
KCBJ—TV, Channel 17,
 501 Business Loop 70 E.
KFRU Radio,
 1911 Business Loop 70 E.
KOMU—TV, Channel 8,
 Highway 63 S.
Karins, Tom (telephone switchman),
 4657 Southhampton
Karlin, Linda D. (social worker),
 1417 Lexington Circle E.
Karnjanapun, Supit (student),
 708A University Village
Kelley Motor Spectrum,
 500 Vandiver Drive.
Kelly, Chris S. (county clerk),
 705 Glenwood Court
Kempf, Arleen (fiscal analyst, University),
 306 W. Broadway
Kettle, Barry & Judy (insurance underwriter),
 1700 Iris Dr.
Keyser, Robert D (student),
 101 Green Meadows Rd, Apt. 101
Kidwell, Donald L. & S. Juanita (Eastgate Party Shop),
 1117 Again St.
Knaebel, Alban F. (Hulett Heating),
 Route 3
Knipp Construction Co.,
 1204 Pannell St.
Knipp, Richard H. (Knipp Constr Co.),
 210 Forest Ave.
Koenig, Richard E. & Corin (KCBJ—TV), addr unk
Kruse, Linda (student),
 201 N. Sixth St.
Kuhlman, John M. (prof, University),
 Rt. 1 Hartsburg

—L—

Lamberti, Joseph W. & Ramona (prof, University),
 1121 Woodhill Rd.
Lang, David P. & Elizabeth S. (mgr, Subrogation Dept),
 309 S. Glenwood Ave.
Law, Deborah (bank clerk),
 211 E. Cherry St.
Lawhorn, James E. (technician, City Electronics),
 801 Schepker
Lear, Truman E. & Laura I. (retired),
 1502 W. Ash St.
Lee, Richard L. (prof, University),
 Route 1
Legg, Phillip N. & Evelyn S. (retired),
 1303 Parkridge Dr.
Lindstrom, David D. (dir, University Y),
 211 E. Glenwood Ave.
Losty, Barbara (dean, Stephens College),
 1026 Westwinds Ct.
Lucas, Lawrence W. and Emily (medical doctor),
 210 Canterbury Dr.
Lusby, Earnestine (secretary, University),
 300 W. Worley St.
Lynch, Sharon (nurse),
 2111 E. Walnut St.
Lyon, Dianne (coach),
 2411 Shepard Blvd.

—M—

Maddox, Gary (policeman),
 1205 University Ave.
McDaniels, Edward (emp unk),
 1305 Elleta Blvd.
McElyea, Ethel M. (retired),
 107 W. Broadway
Mead, Larry E. & Kathleen P. (Editor, *Sheep Breeder* mag), 17 Bingham Rd.
Meade, Carol (student),
 1011 Southpark Dr., Apt. 4
Mermelstein, Albert H. & Joanne (emp Crippled Children's Clinic), 209 Sappington Dr.
Mitchell, Alice L. (retired),
 2 E. Ridgeley Rd.
Mitchell, Herbert L. & Alice R. (emp, Center for Disabilities), 903 E. El Cortez Dr.
Mitchell, Wendell P. & Jeanette (policeman),
 101 W. Texas Ave.
Moore, Dennis (bank teller),
 1315 Ashland Gravel Rd., Apt. G
Moseley, Joseph L. & Carol (county prosecutor),
 1304 Woodhill Rd.
Murrin, Arthur W. & Colleen J. (fire eng, city),
 1300 Dawn Ridge Rd.
Music Shop,
 923 E. Broadway
Myers, Murry R. & Martha A. (Forum Cleaners),
 810 Bourne Ave.

—N—

Nansen, James D. & Mary (doctor),
  330 Bethel St.
Naugle Companies,
  Route 2, Box 138
Neal, Betty J. (sales, Sears),
  203 Ruby Lane
Neal, Paul A. (police det.),
  309 E. Rollins Rd.
Nelson, Roberta H. (secretary),
  2001 Newton Dr.
New American Life Insurance Co.,
  3301 W. Broadway
Newberry, Dan (student),
  205 College Ave.
Newhard Cook & Co., Brokers,
  10 N. Garth Ave.
Nichols, John (switchman, tele co.)
  Route 2 Hallsville
Nicholson, Calvin (student),
  101 Green Meadows Rd., Apt. 38
Ninnenger, Timothy & Bernadette (supply rep),
  Route 4
Noren, Wendy (county clerk),
  3107 Blackberry Lane
Norgetown Laundry,
  Biscayne Mall
Novus Shop Inc., 22 S. 9th St.
Null, Mary Mrs. (retired),
  1201 Paquin St., Apt. 707

—O—

Odor, Raymond W. & Carol A. (tchr-coach, schools),
  2412 Bluff Blvd.
Olson, Laura A. (nurse),
  1203 Stone Court
Orkin Termite & Pest Control,
  1808 Vandiver
Oskins, Perry B. (prof, University),
  1330 Overhill Rd.
Owens, Kenneth & Debbie (city fire engr),
  Rt. 5, Box 344A
Oxenhandler, Brad (student),
  8 Keene St., Apt. K71

—P—

Pa's Bait Shop,
  1304 Wilkes Blvd.
Paulsell, Steve (chief, fire protection dist.),
  Route 5
Perez, Eli C. (analyst, University),
  2302 Walther Court
Perkowski, Mitchell (University),
  605 Fifth St., Apt. D.
Poll, Max H. & Judith (adm, Boone Co. Hosp.),
  1101 Lakeside Dr.
Powell, Albert (Central Electronics),
  1206 Tandy Ave.

Pugh, Robert K. & Connie G. (vice pres, The Book Store), 502 W. Rock Creek Dr.

—R—

Rademacher, Cathy (Hairy's Place),
  3500 N. Stadium Blvd.
Radovich, Clare (cash, Buchroeder's),
  206 Hitt, Apt. 309
Rainey, Thomas G. (mgr Salty's Sandwiches),
  1207 W. Ash St.
Rardin, J.E. & Associates,
  213 Brewer Dr.
Ratliff, Earl D. & Lucille (retired),
  511 Simmons Ct.
Realty World,
  1500 I-70 Dr. S.W.
Redman, Scott (emp unk),
  1030 Southpark Dr., Apt. 2A
Reichenbacher, Barry R. & Martha S. (emp unk),
  207 Pinewood Dr.
Richter, Clifford (chief rad therapist, Ellis Fischel Hosp), 513 Woodridge Dr.
Rikli, Arthur E. & Frances M. (prof, University),
  4003 Faurot Dr.
Ritter, James D. & Patty (asst. schools supt.),
  2190 Birch Road.
Robb's Kerr-McGee,
  103 N. Providence Rd.
Roberts, C. David & Kristy (tchr, University),
  1113 S. Glenwood Ave.
Robinson's Cleaners,
  907 University Ave.
Rojanasuwan, Choochit (student),
  413 Hitt St., Apt. 302
Roshawn, William (emp Masterhosts Inn),
  1225 Elleta Blvd.
Ruffner, Robert (geologist),
  710 Rogers St.
Rweter, Diana (aide, Woodhaven Learning Ctr),
  Business 63 S.

—S—

Sadich, Robert & Mary (dentist),
  211 E. Danforth Dr.
Saiger, Paul & Linda (dir, B'nai B'rith Hillel Found.),
  300 McNab Dr.
Sanford, Michael R. & Marilyn K. (dir, dept. of community services), 3100 Hill Haven Lane
Schaeffer, Hal O. (student),
  101 Green Meadows Rd, Apt. 13
Scott, Patricia (city clerk),
  2110 West Blvd. S.
Simpson, John R. (emp unk),
  2703 Meadowlark Lane
Sletten, Craig (mgr, Iseman Mobile Homes),
  3903 Clark Lane, Lot 123
Smeed, Nick (city personnel dir),
  211 Lynnwood Dr.

Smith & Co., Inc.,
   16 E. Sixth St.
Smith, John (Ellis Fischel Hosp.),
   909 Crawford
Southwest Swim Club,
   211 College Park Dr.
Spangler, Barrett (Burrito T-Shirt Co.),
   1616 Radcliffe Dr.
Stanley, Robert M. (lieutenant, fire dept.),
   2401 W. Broadway
Stephens, Steve M. (police sgt.),
   1203 N. 9th St.
Stoerker, Lewis W. & Dorothy (state sec, Travelers
   Prot. Assn.), 106 College Ave.
Strawn, Estell P. (painting contr),
   120 Pinewood Dr.
Sulzen, James D. & Lisa,
   3900 Clark Lane, Lot 123
Swanson, Herbert C. Rev. & Chloe (Calvary Lutheran
   Church), 1914 Garden Dr.
Sylvester, Steve (student),
   305 Edgewood Ave.

—T—

Taracido, Jorge (emp, University),
   411 Parkade Blvd.
Tarrant, Johnny L. & Loraine E. (chemist),
   1401 Dawn Dr.
Taylor, Larry & Lee (law clerk),
   4600 Oakview Dr.
Teter, Elizabeth (housemother),
   600 E. Rollins St.
Thomann, David W. (student),
   815 Cypress Lane
Thompson, Russell V. & Ruth (supt., city schools),
   Route 4
Thomiere, Nancy J. (emp Mental Health Ctr),
   301 Tiger Lane, Apt. 208
Thompson, Nancy J. (bookkeeper, Adams Constr),
   Fulton
Tibbs, Joyce L. (clk Utilities Co.),
   21 Sunset Trailer Ct.
Tillema, Herbert K. & Susan M.
   (assoc prof, University),
   306 Westridge Dr.
Tolksdorf, Christina M. (student),
   1405 Bouchelle Ave.
Trautwein, Erwin L. & Mary H. (retired),
   2 Miller Dr.
Tritschler, Ralph & Billie (construction worker),
   2110 E. Cardinal Dr.
Turner, Charles S. & Anna L. (retired),
   906 Charles St.
Turner, Shirley J. (custodian),
   Route 3

—U—

United Parcel Service,
   2501 Vandiver Drive

United Way,
   Strollway Centre
University Y,
   308 Read Hall
Urban, David L. & Leslie Ann (The Creative Eye),
   2207 Bear Creek Dr.

—V—

VIP Travel Service,
   101 W. Broadway
Valentine, A. Merrill & Juanita (Christman Jewelry),
   111 Dawn Dr.
Vining, Victor E. (supervisor, University),
   P.O. Box 219
Vogt, Christi N. (bank teller),
   1509 Paris Rd.

—W—

Wagahoff, Adeline (clerk),
   1408 Parkade Blvd.
Walls, Richard L. & Joyce (Heidelberg restnt),
   10 McGregor Lane
Walsh, David E. & Georgene (emp city),
   27 E. Thurman St.
Warren, David S. & Doris (computer analyst),
   2 Comanche Ct.
Watkins, Paul A. & Rose T. (Paul Watkins Co.),
   104 Orr St.
Webber, Jonathan T. & Wendy (asst, University),
   2221 Concordia St.
Wendy's Old Fashioned Hamburgers,
   200 Business Loop 70 W.
Westlund, John D. & Janet L. (pres Real Estate Ctr),
   2809 Biscayne Ct.
Williams, Pearl Mrs. (retired),
   219 Unity Dr.
Willows, Jay & Peggy (dir, vocational education,
   public schools), 1214 N. Garth Ave.
Windmiller, Eugene & Perva L. (phys),
   1502 E. Broadway
Windmiller, Myrl E. (firefighter),
   Route 1
Wood, Glenn (retired),
   110 S. Garth Ave.
Woolford, Lyn (sheriff's deputy),
   2110 W. Southpark Dr.
Wright, Hewitt P. & Lynn A. (emp Amdahl Corp.),
   900 Lynwood Ct.
Wright, Marvin E. & Janet (atty),
   1109 Pheasant Run Dr.
Wu, Kung Yao (student),
   1205 University Ave.

—Y—

Yaeger, Bob (D&H Enterprises),
   2009 Wolcott Dr.
Yates, Virgil T. & Janet B. (adm Ellis Fischel Hosp.),
   1704 Princeton Dr.

Yeargin, Howard R. (carpenter),
	Route 9
Yeargin, Marge N. (emp unk),
	Route 7
Yeargin, Russell B. (salesman),
	3435 E. William St.
Young, Toni D. (nurse),
	100 Keene St., Apt. 10

Yowell, Ruby M. (retired),
	902 Rogers St.

—Z—

Zimmerman, Roger (student),
	3212 Woodbine Dr.
Zwonitzer, Wilbur E. (contractor),
	1524 West Blvd. S.

APPENDIX IV

STREET INDEX

—A—

Again Street
Alameda Court
Alan Lane
Aldeah Avenue
Alexander Avenue
Alfred Street
Alhambra Drive
Allen Street
Alsup Drive
Alton Avenue
Amelia Street
Ammonette Street
Anderson Avenue
Andy Drive
Ann Street
Anthony Street
Arapahoe Circle
Arapahoe Place
Arbor Drive
Argyle Road
Arlington Street
Ash Street
Ashland Gravel Road
Ashley Street
Aspen Drive
Aster Court
Atkins Drive
Auburn Lane
Audubon Drive
Austin Avenue
Aztec Boulevard

—B—

Balboa Lane
Ballenger Place
Ballenger Lane
Balow Wynd
Banks Avenue
Barberry Avenue
Barkley Avenue
Bass Avenue
Bayonne Court
Beachview Drive
Bear Creek Drive
Belle Meade Drive
Belleview Court
Belmont Street
Benton Street
Bernadette Drive
Berrywood Drive
Bethel Street
Bettina Drive
Beulah Drive
Beverly Drive
Bicknell Street
Big Bear Boulevard
Birch Road
Bingham Road
Biscayne Court
Bittersweet Court
Blackberry Lane
Blackfoot Road
Blair Court

Blossom Court
Blue Ridge Road
Bluff Boulevard
Bluff Dale Drive
Bob-O-Link Drive
Bonny Linn Drive
Bowling Street
Bouchelle Avenue
Bourn Avenue
Boyd Lane
Bradford Drive
Bradshaw Avenue
Braemore Road
Brandon Road
Bray Avenue
Brenda Lane
Brewer Drive
Brighton Street
Bristol Court
Broadhead Street
Broadway
Brookside Court
Brown's Station Rd.
Bruin Street
Bryant Street
Buckner Street
Bucks Run
Burlington Street
Burnam Avenue
Burnam Road
Burrwood Drive
Bushnell Drive

—C—

Calico Lane
Calvert Drive
Calvin Drive
Cambridge Drive
Camino Real
Caniff Circle
Canterbury Drive
Canyon Drive
Cardinal Drive
Carolyn Avenue
Carpenter Drive
Casa Circle
Cedar Cliff Drive
Cedar Lane
Chalmers Road
Chandler Court
Chantilly Court
Charles Street
Cherokee Lane
Cherry Street
Chestnut Street
Chickasaw Drive
Christian College Avenue
Circus Avenue
Clark Lane
Clarkson Road
Claudell Lane
Clayton Street
Cliff Drive
Clinkscales Road
Clinton Drive

Coats Street
Colby Drive
Colgate
College Avenue
College Park Drive
Colonial Court
Colorado Avenue
Comanche Court
Concord Street
Concordia Drive
Condado Court
Conley Avenue
Conley Road
Cook Avenue
Cornell
Corte Hermoso
Corte Nuevo
Cosmos Place
Cottle Drive
Country Club Drive
Country Club Drive S.
Country Lane
Country Side Lane
Court Street
Coventry Lane
Covington Place
Cowan Drive
Craig Street
Crawford Street
Creasy Springs Road
Crescent Road
Crestland Avenue
Crestmere Avenue
Crestridge Drive
Crown Point
Crump Lane
Curtis Avenue
Cypress Lane

—D—

Dahlia Drive
Dakota Avenue
Danforth Circle
Danforth Court
Danforth Drive
Dartmouth
Davis Street
Dawn Ridge Road
Dean Street
Deer Run Drive
Defoe Court
Defoe Drive
Derek Court
Devine Court
Diamond Avenue
Dogwood Lane
Donnelly Avenue
Dorado Drive
Doris Drive
Dorsey Street
Dover Avenue
Duke Street
Duncan Street
Dundee Drive
Dysart Street

—E—

East Ash Street
East Boulevard
East Briarwood Lane
East Henley Drive
East Lexington Circle
East Parkway Drive
East Rockcreek Drive
East Sugar Tree Lane
East Walnut Street
East Willowbrook Road
Eastlake Drive
Eastland Circle
Eastwood Circle
Eastwood Drive
Edgewood Avenue
Edison Street
Edris Drive
Edwards Court
Eighth Street
El Cortez Drive
Eldorado Court
Eldorado Drive
Elleta Boulevard
Elliott Drive
Ellis Court
Elm Street
Elm Grove Drive
Elmview Drive
Essex Court
Eubank Court
Eugenia Street
Eva Drive
Evans Road
Evergreen Lane

—F—

Fair Haven Drive
Fair Lane
Fairmont
Fairview Avenue
Fairview Road
Fairway Drive
Falcon Drive
Faurot Drive
Fay Street
Fellows Drive
Fellows Place
Field Crest
Fifth Street
Fir Place
First Street
Fleetwood Drive
Flora Drive
Florence Avenue
Florida Court
Forest Avenue
Forest Hill Court
Fourth Street
Frances Drive
Fredora Avenue
Fulton Road
Fyfer Place

—G—

Garden Court
Garden Drive
Garnet Avenue
Garnet Drive
Garth Avenue
Gary Street
Gentry Avenue
George Court
Georgetown Drive
Gipson Court
Gipson Street
Glenn Drive
Glenwood Avenue
Glenwood Court
Glorietta Drive
Gordon Street
Grace Ellen Drive
Granada Boulevard
Grand Avenue
Grant Lane
Greeley Drive
Greeley Street
Greenwood Avenue
Greenwood Court
Green Meadows Road
Green Ridge Road
Green Valley Drive
Grindstone Avenue
Grissum Drive
Guitar Street

—H—

Haden Drive
Hamilton Way
Hardin Street
Hartley Court
Harvard
Hathman Place
Hatton Drive
Haven Road
Hawthorne Drive
Hazelwood Drive
Heather Lane
Heidman Road
Hendrix Drive
Henley Court
Heriford Road
Hickam Drive
Hickman Avenue
Hickory Hill Drive
Hickory Street
High Street
Highland Drive
Highridge Circle
Highridge Drive
Highview Avenue
Hill Haven Lane
Hillcrest Road
Hillside Drive
Hinkson Avenue
Hinkson Creek Road
Hirth Avenue
Hitt Street

Hodge Street
Holly Avenue
Hominy Branch Court
Honeysuckle Drive
Hope Place
Hubbell Drive
Hulen Drive
Hunt Avenue
Hunt Court

—I—

I-70 Drive N.W.
I-70 Drive S.E.
I-70 Drive S.W.
Illinois Avenue
Independence Street
Indiana Avenue
Industrial Drive
Ingleside Drive
Iowa Avenue
Iris Drive
Isherwood Circle
Isherwood Drive
Ivy Way

—J—

Jackson Street
Jake Lane
James Dale Road
Jean Rae Drive
Jefferson Street
Jewell Avenue
Joann Street
Johnson Drive
Jolene
June Lane
Juniper Court
Juniper Drive
Juniper Place

—K—

Kathy Drive
Keene Court
Keene Street
Kensington Road
Kentucky Boulevard
King Avenue
Knipp Street
Kohler Drive
Kraemer Court
Kuhlman Court

—L—

LaGrange Road
Lake of the Woods Road
Lake Street
Lakeshore Drive
Lakeside Drive
Lakeview Avenue
Lambeth Drive
Lamp Lane
Lancaster Drive

Lansing Avenue
Laoris Street
Larch Court
Lasalle Place
Lathrop Road
Laurel Drive
Lawrence Place
Lawnridge Court
Leawood Terrace
Lee Street
Leeway Drive
Lenoir Street
Leslie Lane
Lexington Court
Liberty Street
Lightview Drive
Lilac Drive
Lilly Court
Limerick Lane
Lindell Drive
Lindy Lane
Loch Lane
Locust Street
Loma Court
London Drive
Longfellow Lane
Longwell Drive
Lovejoy Lane
Lowe Street
Lowry Street
Luan Court
Lucas Way
Lucerne Court
Lynn Street
Lynnwood Drive
Lyon Street

—M—

McAlester Street
McBaine Avenue
McGregor Lane
McKee Street
Madera Drive
Madison Street
Madrid Lane
Magnolia Court
Malibu Court
Mallard Court
Manor Court
Manor Drive
Maplewood Drive
Marion Drive
Marsha Court
Martha Drive
Martin Drive
Mary Street
Marygene Street
Mary Jane Drive
Maryland Avenue
Marylee Drive
Matthews Street
Maupin Road
Meadow Lane
Meadowlark Lane
Meadowvale Court

Medavista Drive
Mehl Road
Melbourne Street
Melody Lane
Mesa Drive
Mexico Gravel Road
Middlebush Drive
Mikel Street
Millbrook Drive
Mimosa Court
Miramar Lane
Mission Court
Missouri Avenue
Mitchell Court
Mizzou Place
Mohawk Avenue
Mohawk Court
Monroe Street
Monterey Drive
Moon Valley Road
Morning Glory Drive
Moss Street
Mt. Vernon Avenue
Mulberry Road
Mumford Drive
Murrell Drive

—N—

Navaho Avenue
Nebraska Avenue
Nelwood Drive
New Haven Avenue
Newton Drive
Nichols Street
Nifong Boulevard
Ninth Street
Noble Court
Norma Court
North Boulevard
North Circle
Northridge Drive
North Parklawn Court
North Valley View Drive
North Wappel Drive
North Willowbrook Road
Northland Drive

—O—

Oak Forest Drive
Oak Lawn Drive
Oak Street
Oakhaven Drive
Oakland Gravel Road
Oakland Place
Oakview Drive
Oakwood Court
Oakwood Drive
Olive Street
Onofrio Court
Orange Street
Orchard Court
Orchard Lane
Oriole Lane
Orleans Court

Orr Street
Otto Court
Overhill Court
Overhill Road
Oxford
Oyama Street

—P—

Pannell Street
Paris Court
Paris Road
Park Avenue
Park DeVille Drive
Park Hill Avenue
Parkade Boulevard
Parker Street
Parklawn Court
Parklawn Drive
Parkridge Court
Parkridge Drive
Parkside Drive
Parkview Drive
Paseo Hermoso
Patsy Lane
Paquin Street
Pearl Avenue
Pecan Street
Pendleton Street
Pennant Street
Pennsylvania Drive
Perkins Drive
Pershing Road
Petite Court
Pheasant Run Drive
Phyllis Avenue
Pickford Place
Pierre Street
Pin Oak Court
Pine Drive
Pinecrest Drive
Pinewood Drive
Pioneer Drive
Planter Road
Plaza Drive
Pleasant Way
Plymouth Drive
Ponderosa Street
Poplar Street
Porter Street
Portland Street
Powell Drive
Powell Lane
Prairie Lane
Prairie Ridge Street
Prairie View Drive
Pratt Street
Price Avenue
Primrose Drive
Princeton Drive
Proctor Drive
Prospect Street
Providence Road

—Q—

Quail Drive

Queen Ann Drive
Quisenberry Drive

—R—

Radcliffe Drive
Randy Lane
Range Line Street
Readosa Lane
Red Oak Lane
Redbud Lane
Redwood Road
Rhonda Lane
Riback Road
Rice Road
Richardson Street
Richland Road
Richmond Avenue
Rider Avenue
Ridge Road
Ridgefield Road
Ridgeley Road
Ridgemont
Ridgemont Court
Ridgeway Avenue
Riney Lane
Ripley Street
Riveria Drive
Robert Ray Court
Robert Ray Drive
Rock Quarry Road
Rock Wood Place
Rockhamton Circle
Rockhill Road
Rockingham Drive
Rogers Street
Rollingwood Drive
Rollins Road
Rollins Street
Roosevelt Avenue
Rose Cliff Drive
Rose Court
Rose Drive
Rosemary Lane
Ross Street
Rothwell Drive
Rowe Lane
Rowland Road
Ruby Lane
Russell Boulevard
Rustic Road
Rutledge Drive
Rye Lane

—S—

St. Andrew Street
St. Ann Court
St. Charles Road
St. Christopher Street
St. James Street
St. Joseph Street
St. Michael Drive
Sandifer Avenue
Sanford Avenue
Sanford Street

—290—

Santiago Drive	Spring Hill Road	Thilly Avenue	Vista Place	Weymeyer Drive
Sappington Drive	Spring Valley Road	Third Avenue		Wheaton Court
Schwabe Lane	Spruce Drive	Thistledown Drive	—W—	White Gate Drive
Scott Boulevard	Squire Circle	Thornhill Road		White Oak Lane
Sears Court	Stadium Boulevard	Thurman Street	Wabash Drive	Wilde Drive
Second Street	Stalcup Street	Tiger Lane	Waco Road	Wilkes Boulevard
Seneca Avenue	Stanford Drive	Timber Hill Road	Walcox Drive	William Street
Seventh Street	Starke Avenue	Timber Hill Trail	Wales	Willis Avenue
Seville Avenue	Starlight Drive	Tipton Terrace	Wallace Street	Willow Way
Sexton Road	Stephen Drive	Topaz Drive	Walnut Street	Willowbrook Court
Seymour Road	Stevendave Drive	Towne Drive	Walther Court	Wilson Avenue
Shannon Place	Stewart Road	Tracy Drive	Warwick Street	Windmill Court
Shepard Boulevard	Stone Street	Tremaine Drive	Washington Avenue	Windsor Street
Shepard Court	Stoney Lane	Trinity Place	Waterford Court	Wolfcreek Court
Sherwood Drive	Stony Brook Place	Troyer Drive	Waterford Drive	Wood Hill Road
Sheryl Drive	Strawn Road	Truman Drive	Waterloo Drive	Woodbine Drive
Shockley Street	Subella Drive	Tulip Court	Watson Place	Woodkirk Drive
Short Street	Summit Road	Tupelo Place	Waugh Street	Woodkirk Lane
Sierra Madre	Sunflower Street	Turner Avenue	Wayne Road	Woodland Drive
Silvey Street	Sunset Drive	Turner Drive	Wayside Drive	Woodlawn Avenue
Simmons Court	Sunset Lane	Twin Oak Court	Wee Wynd	Woodlea Drive
Sims Street	Surfside Court	Twin Oak Drive	West Boulevard Court	Woodrail Avenue
Sinclair Street	Switzler Street		West Boulevard North	Woodrail Terrace
Sixth Street	Sycamore Lane	—U—	West Boulevard South	Woodridge Court
Skye Wynd	Sylvan Lane		West Briarwood Lane	Woodridge Drive
Skylark Drive		University Avenue	West Henley Drive	Woodridge Road
Skyview Road	—T—		West Lexington Circle	Woodrow Street
Smarr Court		—V—	West Parkway Drive	Woods Court
Smiley Lane	Taft Street		West Rockcreek Drive	Woodside Drive
Smith Street	Tahoe Court	Valencia Drive	West Sugar Tree Lane	Woodson Way
Sondra Avenue	Tammy Lane	Valley Court	West Walnut Court	Worley Street
South Country Club Drive	Tandy Avenue	Valley View Road	Westmount Avenue	Wyatt Lane
South Drive	Tara Lane	Vandiver Drive	Westover Street	Wyoming Avenue
South Eastwood Circle	Taylor Street	Vassar	Westport Drive	
South Wappel Drive	Teal Drive	Vegas Drive	Westridge Drive	—Y—
Southhampton Drive	Tejon Circle	Victoria Drive	Westwind Drive	
Southpark Drive	Tenth Street	Vine Street	Westwinds Court	Yale
Southridge Drive	Terry Lane	Violet Court	Westwinds Drive	Yorktown Drive
Southwood Drive	Texas Avenue	Virginia Avenue	Westwood Avenue	Yuma Drive
Spencer Avenue				

APPENDIX V

PAGE LAYOUT AIDS

DATE 4/24 PAGE 1A

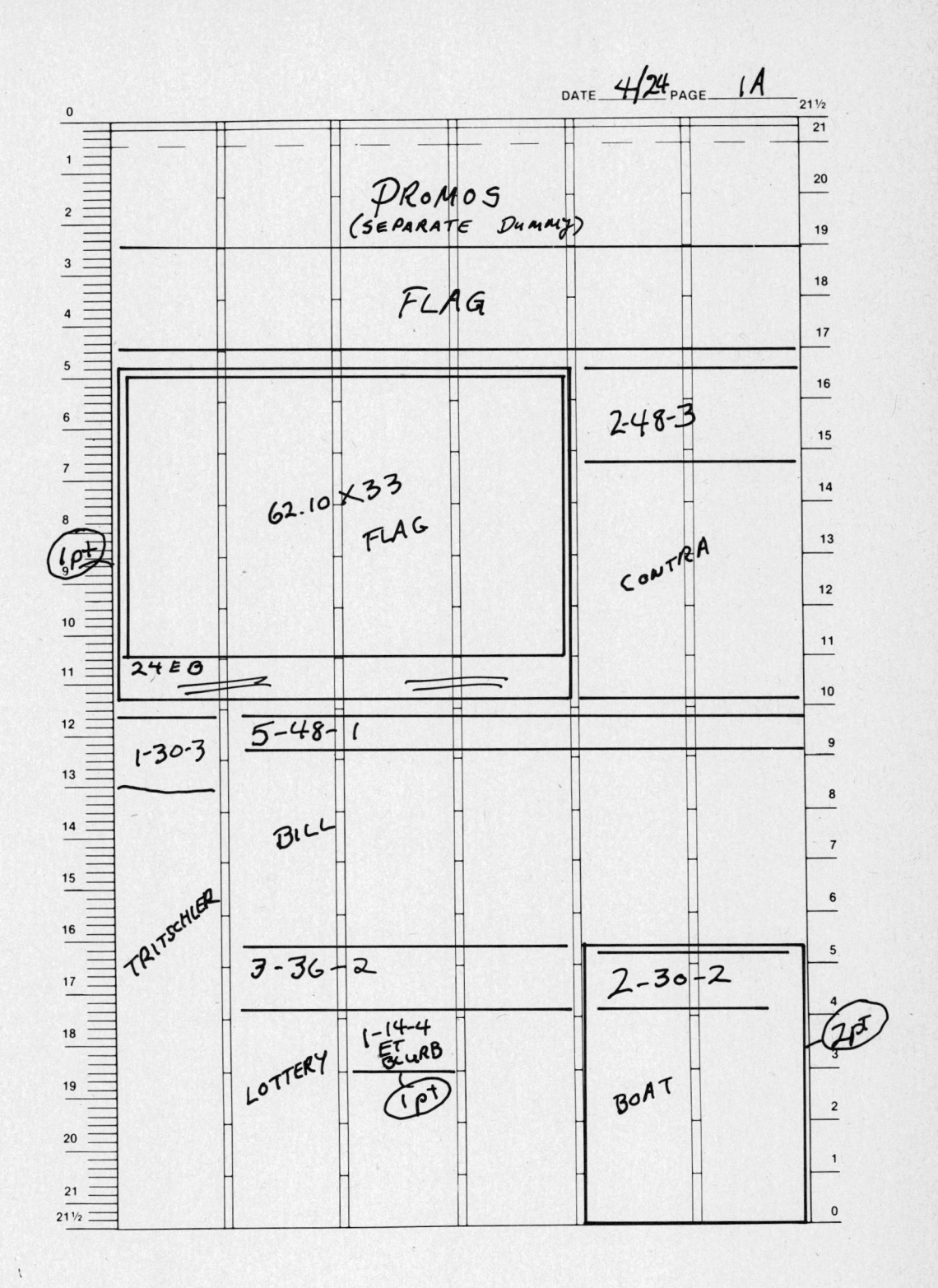

PROMOS
(SEPARATE DUMMY)

FLAG

62.10 × 33
FLAG

24 E O

2-48-3
CONTRA

1-30-3
TRITSCHLER

5-48-1
BILL

3-36-2
LOTTERY

1-14-4
ET BLURB
(1pt)

2-30-2
BOAT

(1pt)

(2J)

Dutch touch

'If you aren't Dutch, you aren't much,' claims an old Dutch saying, reflecting Holland's sense of pride about its cooking. Find recipes for olie bollen, flensjes, erwtensoep and Gouda asparagus rolls on **Food, Page 1B.**

That's a winner

Tiger shortstop Tom Ciombor was long on heroics Tuesday night. His single in the ninth inning gave Missouri a 5-4 victory over the University of Missouri-Rolla. The Tigers are now 30-17. **See Sports, Page 8A.**

Is Coke still it?

Coca-Cola, the world's top-selling soft drink for almost a century, is changing its recipe to make it 'smoother and sweeter,' company officials said Tuesday. Read about the new strategy on today's **Business, Page 1E.**

The Daily Constitution

76th Year — No. 188 | Good Morning! It's Wednesday, April 24 | 11 Sections — 66 Pages — 25 Cents

Scott Takushi

Groundwork

Kathleen Regan of Chi Omega and Steve Meyer of Pi Kappa Alpha are bent on finishing a yard-sized flag for use during Greek Week, which begins Saturday. They worked on the Pikes' lawn at 916 Providence Road this week to prepare the banner for use as a backdrop for the two houses' fling presentation to be held in Jesse Auditorium.

Senate passes, House defeats contra aid plan

WASHINGTON (UPI) — The House Tuesday defeated President Reagan's proposal for $14 million in aid to Nicaragua's contra rebels, handing the administration its biggest foreign-policy defeat.

But the administration, armed with the earlier approval of the plan in the Republican-controlled Senate, vowed to return to fight another day, and maneuvered behind a compromise drawn up by House Republican leader Robert Michel of Illinois.

Reagan won Senate approval 53-46 after compromising with Senate Democrats on two controversial points. Sen. John Danforth, R-Mo., voted for the plan, and Sen. Thomas Eagleton, D-Mo., voted against it.

The House defeated the plan 180-248.

The next showdown on the aid to the rebels, who are committed to the overthrow of Nicaragua's Marxist-led Sandinista government, was scheduled for Wednesday when the House votes on a liberal Democratic counter-aid proposal and the Michel plan.

The Tuesday night votes in Congress — just over an hour apart — wound up a daylong debate in the two Houses, where a Senate-led drive for a compromise collapsed shortly after noon.

But before the vote, Reagan won the votes of 10 Senate Democrats by giving in on resuming direct negotiations between Washington and the Managua government and extending until September the time period the money would go only for humanitarian purposes.

Reagan had no comment on the House defeat but issued a statement immediately after the Senate vote, saying: "Tonight, the Senate cast an historic vote — for freedom and democracy in Central America."

The main hangup left appeared to be Reagan's unstated role for the CIA in distributing the money. The administration suggested this may be through the oversight of the National Security Council.

Liberal House Democrats want any money administered by forces outside Nicaragua so it cannot be used for arms, while under the Michel plan it would be administered by the Agency for International Development.

In the final House vote, 40 Democrats joined 140 Republicans in voting for the aid bill, while 208 Democrats and 40 Republicans voted against it. Missouri's Republicans voted for the bill, while the state's Democrats voted against it.

Tritschler wins nod by one vote

By Brad Gentry
Missourian staff writer

Doubting the party loyalty of a selection committee's recommendation for presiding commissioner, Boone County Republican Central Committee members Tuesday gave only a one-vote margin of victory for candidate Billie Tritschler.

After two rounds of voting and a pair of recesses, Tritschler won out

Democrat's choice ...Page 13A

over Gene Cunnningham, whom the screening committee bypassed at a meeting Saturday.

The split left some members wondering if Republican Gov. John Ashcroft would pick a Democrat for the post.

The selection committee, composed of six members, Saturday voted to recommend the 58-year-old Tritschler for the position, but nearly half of the central committee had other ideas.

The almost two-hour meeting Tuesday produced charges that the selection committee made the pick underhandedly. "The bylaws were not carried through any of this operation," complained former county chairman Grace Edwards.

Cunningham, a former state director of the Agriculture Stabilization and Conservation Service, and Norman Lampton, a Columbia attorney, made pitches for the post, but in the end it was Tritschler who won on a 16-15 vote of the committee.

Before the first round of voting, Cunningham of Route 6 said he sought the position on "qualifications and not cronyism" and cited his political experience — an unsuccessful 1984 campaign for state representative. That is in stark contrast, he said, to Tritschler's lack of political activity.

"I would ask you to nominate the best candidate," he said.

In one last salvo, Cunningham said if Tritschler were selected, he "would welcome her as an active Republican."

Candidate Lampton added fuel to

See GOP, Page 14A

Bill would give M.U. $240 million plus

By Charles Phillips and Peggy L. Davis
State capital bureau

JEFFERSON CITY — It only took the Missouri House a minute and a half Tuesday to give preliminary approval to an appropriations bill for higher education. The bill would give the University of Missouri system more than $240 million.

Earlier in the day, the House approved a $120 million increase — a 14 percent boost — in state aid to local public schools. Of the $120 million, $20 million is a one-time appropriation.

The House-passed budget would provide a $20 million increase in funds for the University of Missouri's general operating budget.

Included in the $240 million are one-time appropriations of $7 million to buy computer equipment and $5.9 million for library acquisitions.

The House also approved $550,000 to implement the second year of a research project, Food for the 21st Century, which is designed to put Missouri in the forefront of new technologies for food production.

Since the legislature can't earmark funds to specific divisions of the University system, a $1 million appropriation to the College of Veterinary Medicine was included in the general operating expenses.

Rep. Everett Brown, D-Maryville and sponsor of the bill, said during House debate a letter of intent would be sent to the University requesting the money be used for the veterinary medicine program. He also said University of Missouri President Peter Magrath already has sent the legislature a letter of intent.

Rep. Chris Kelly, D-Columbia, said: "I was very pleased. We got a real fine appropriation for the University."

The $205 million is a compromise between the $223 million the Department of Higher Education requested and the $199 million that Gov. John Ashcroft reccommended.

The House also approved $14.8 million for University Hospital; $532,000 for the State Historical Society; $3.9 million for renal disease research; and $2.1 million for the Institute of Psychiatry in St. Louis.

In other action, House Budget Committee Chairman Marvin Proffer, D-Jackson, recommended Tuesday the University four-campus system get $24 million for building maintenance, repair and renovation projects.

Proffer's recommendation would provide $12.8 million for the Columbia campus.

The recommendations do not cover new building construction projects Proffer plans to propose to the House Budget Committee Thursday.

Included in Proffer's Tuesday recommendations for the Columbia campus are:

$4.6 million for a new turbine generator at the power plant; $7.1 million for maintenance and repair projects; $963,000 for campus handicap accessibility projects; $1.04 million for maintenance and repair projects at the University Hospital; $612,500 for renovating the hospital's pediatric and intermediate intensive-care unit; $200,000 for handicap accessibility projects at the hospital; and $1.5 million in maintenance and repair funds for the University agriculture experiment station.

Proffer said he plans to vote the bill out of the committee by Monday, when it will be sent to the full House for its consideration.

Compromise lottery bill's fate hinges on taxation of winnings

By Kathryn Kranhold
State capital bureau

JEFFERSON CITY — The lottery showdown is almost over.

After weeks of debate, Rep. Karen McCarthy, D-Kansas City, and Sen. Ed Dirck, D-St. Louis, appear to have worked out most of their grievances in a bill that would put the lottery machinery in motion upon signature by Gov. John Ashcroft.

Despite the possible truce, both parties say they've given up a lot.

"I've made more compromises than necessary," Dirck said.

McCarthy has similar feelings: "We can't give them any more than we have already."

Only one provision remains to be decided — should lottery winnings totaling more than $600 be taxed by the state. The House wants to tax winnings in accordance with the state statute on taxing gambling winnings. The Senate, specifically bill-sponsor Dirck, wants no taxation of prizes.

According to a report by the Department of Revenue, the state could lose more than $12 million without the state tax.

Dirck contends "there will be no income tax" regardless of the state statute. If he has his way, no lottery bill will be passed this year under the House's plan to assess a state tax.

> The bill's sponsor, Sen. Ed Dirck, D-St. Louis, doesn't want winnings taxed.

"We'll have to come back next year," Dirck said.

"He (Dirck) shouldn't throw the whole bill into jeopardy because of the tax," McCarthy said.

McCarthy submitted Tuesday the House's final compromise to Dirck with the required signatures from the five House members on the conference committee. But Dirck refused to sign the bill because of the income tax provision.

In order to pass the bill through both houses, the bill must be signed by eight of the 10 members of the conference committee. Following approval by Ashcroft and the General Assembly, a three-person commission will be appointed by Ashcroft to oversee the lottery.

Other provisions worked out by Dirck and McCarthy involve qualifications for lottery retailers and the type of lottery games Missourians will be able to play.

Under the compromise version, the non-existent lottery commission will decide what type of games will be played, providing the games do not have themes of horse racing, dog racing or casino games, such as blackjack or craps.

Dirck fought for no restrictions on lottery games.

Lottery retailer qualifications in the bill state that retailers may not have been convicted of a felony or be under the age of 21. For the instant lottery, which requires no computer system, anyone who applies will receive a license. To acquire a license for the "big money" games, retailers will have to purchase or rent the necessary equipment and maintain a minimum amount of sales.

Even with the final lottery compromise still pending, McCarthy said she is hopeful.

"I'd still like to have it on the governor's desk by the end of the month," she said.

Japanese fishing boat seized by Soviet vessel

ANCHORAGE, Alaska (UPI) — A Soviet naval vessel seized a Japanese fishing boat with an American woman observer aboard in the Bering Sea near a disputed tract claimed by both the U.S. and Russian governments, officials said Tuesday.

The seized vessel was the Fukuho-Maru No. 18, which was authorized to fish for pollock in an Ohio-size area known as the Navarin Basin.

The vessel carried a woman observer from the National Marine Fisheries Service, which monitors foreign fishing operations within the U.S. 200-mile limit, officials said. It was not known if the vessel actively was fishing when seized.

A State Department spokesman said efforts were under way to secure the release of the American, whose identity was not given.

Coast Guard Petty Officer Dan Dewell said, "We got a report from (another) Japanese fishing vessel around 4:30 in the morning (Tuesday) and what they told us was the Russian navy had boarded the vessel ... and apparently had it under tow. The vessel making this report said they could not establish communications with the Fukuho."

Authorities did not immediately know how many crew members were aboard the fishing vessel, which is a 180-foot stern trawler whose listed owner is Marue Suisan Co. Ltd. of Japan.

The Coast Guard dispatched a C-130 to establish the vessel's exact position, which was reported to be 180 nautical miles west of St. Matthew Island.

"Based on the information we have, it appears the vessel was (within) the 200-mile limit ... However, the U.S. and Soviets have technical differences over the precise (location) of the convention line," said State Department spokesman Mike Sifter.

The dispute centers on the way the 1,800-mile long 1867 Convention line was drawn. An area roughly 225 miles long by 25 miles wide is contested by both superpowers.

There was no immediate response from officials in Moscow.

DATE 4/24 PAGE 6

WORLD

2-36-2

ITALY

1-14-5
ET
EURO
(1pt)

24.4×25
ITALY

2-36-2

JET

2-30-2

SOVIET

12 BF

4-36-1

CHERNENKO

BRIEFLY
1-14-2

GRENADA

1-14-1

AQUINO

5×13
BC BANK

1-14-1

ROYAL

1-14-1

KIM

WORLD

Dozens buried after building falls in Italy

CASTELLANETA, Italy (UPI) — An apartment building weakened by heavy rain collapsed Thursday, killing at least 25 people and leaving dozens more buried in the rubble.

The tall yellow building in the hilltop village that was the hometown of movie legend Rudolph Valentino crumbled like a pack of cards around 4 a.m. Fourteen hours later, authorities said they had recovered 25 bodies and expressed fears that at least 30 more people were still buried in the debris.

"We fear the toll will be very serious," a spokesman for the prefect (regional governor) in nearby Taranto said. "Members of 18 to 20 families were buried under the wreckage."

Among the bodies recovered were three children.

Nine residents were hospitalized for injuries in the early hours after the accident but only one was listed in serious condition.

Police used dogs to sniff out victims beneath the wreckage. Rescuers were unable to use bulldozers and earth removers for fear of killing injured people trapped under the wreckage or toppling the part of the building that remained standing. So they scrabbled in the debris with their bare hands, picks and shovels.

Rescue work by personnel from nearby military bases and hundreds of firefighters and police was stalled during the afternoon while firefighters demolished a dangerously tottering wall.

Hundreds of villagers gathered outside the church of the Immaculate Heart of Mary to watch the rescue operations. They told reporters that for some time there had been doubts about the stability of the 30-year-old building.

"Since last year when they started work to rebuild the sidewalk outside the apartment building, the street turned into a river every time there was heavy rain," one resident said. "The owner of the building had even appointed a lawyer to seek help from local authorities in consolidating the structure."

Castellaneta, a small hill town 25 miles northwest of the Italian naval base and seaport of Taranto, on the heel of the Italian boot, is famed as the home of Valentino, the Hollywood heartthrob of silent movies.

Valentino was born in Castellaneta in 1895 and emigrated to the United States with his family in 1913. He died in 1926. A statue of him stands in the center of the town.

The tall building in the village where movie star Rudolph Valentino was born crumbled like a pack of cards.

Castellaneta, Italy, residents dig through wreckage. *UPI Telephoto*

Gunmen surrender after seizing jetliner

BEIRUT, Lebanon (UPI) — Gunmen seeking freedom for jailed confederates seized a Cyprus Airways jetliner at Beirut airport Thursday and threatened to kill 12 hostages one by one before surrendering peacefully five hours later, Lebanese officials said.

Moslem-run Mourabitoun radio said the ordeal ended when the five Shiite Moslem gunmen climbed down from the plane, leaving their unharmed hostages behind under an agreement for the release of two Lebanese hijackers imprisoned in Cyprus.

The gunmen "withdrew to an undisclosed location," Christian radio said, indicating they might not have been arrested.

In Nicosia, sources close to the Cypriot government said the two Lebanese prisoners would not be released immediately but their case would be reviewed.

The five gunmen had given the Cypriot government a 12-hour ultimatum, saying they would begin killing their captives one by one Friday morning unless Cyprus freed the two convicted hijackers, Lebanese security sources said.

Among the hostages were nine Cyprus Airways crew members, including Swedish captain Steve Wisting, and three Lebanese workers for KLM, the Dutch airline.

"The three Lebanese employees of KLM were standing next to the Cyprus Airways aircraft at the start of the incident and were taken aboard to join the nine crew members," an airport spokesman said.

Officials said four men carrying hand grenades and semi-automatic weapons stormed the plane shortly before it was to leave for Larnaca, Cyprus, and ordered the pilot to taxi to the end of a runway.

Soviet Union confirms crashes; up to 230 dead

MOSCOW (UPI) — A Soviet aviation official said Thursday two recent Aeroflot plane crashes — believed to have killed as many as 230 people — are under investigation and that steps will be taken to avert future air disasters.

"Local newspapers reported the accidents in Minsk and Omsk," Ivan Vasin, deputy minister of civil aviation, told a news conference marking Aeroflot Day. "We are not trying to hide them.

"In both cases, a commission was established to investigate the causes," Vasin said. "The reasons will be found out and appropriate preventive measures will be taken."

The statement from Vasin marked the first Soviet confirmation that an Aeroflot jetliner crashed ir the Siberian city of Omsk last fall. He gave no further details but 150 people were believed killed in the crash.

On Oct. 20, 1984, French travelers who had changed planes in Omsk told Western correspondents that a Tu-154 collided with a fuel truck as it landed in Omsk, bursting into flames and killing all 150 passengers aboard.

At the time, Soviet officials said they had no knowledge of the accident, believed to have been the third worst in Soviet history.

Vasin said the crash in Omsk was reported in local newspapers when it occurred. The Siberian city is closed to foreigners and its newspapers are not available to Western reporters in Moscow.

Moscow rarely acknowledges aviation disasters unless foreigners or high-level Soviet officials are involved. And even then it only releases minimal details.

Chernenko talks to Politburo, say Soviets

MOSCOW (UPI) — President Konstantin Chernenko, after 42 days in seclusion because of illness, emerged Thursday to addressed the ruling Politburo on the need for improved agricultural production, the Tass news agency said.

Tass said the 73-year-old Soviet leader stressed the importance of the spring crop, which has been substandard for the past six years.

The Tass report was read on national television but was not accompanied by pictures or videotape of the meeting.

Chernenko's six-week absence prompted rumors he had suffered a serious health problem. Speculation on the nature of the rumored ailment included a stroke, heart attack and pneumonia. Soviet officials on several occasions confirmed Chernenko was ill but declined to give details.

In the latest reports, the London Evening Standard said the Soviet leader was recovering from a "massive" heart attack. And the editor of Pravda told an Italian television station Chernenko was ill but could still carry out his duties.

Chernenko's presence at the regular Thursday meeting of the 11-member Politburo was mentioned in the fifth paragraph of the Tass report.

The news agency regularly publishes notes on Politburo sessions that are read on the television news without pictures.

Chernenko is next scheduled to appear in public Feb. 22 or 23 to deliver an election speech ending a campaign for seats in the Supreme Soviet of the Russian Republic.

BRIEFLY

American, other forces to leave Grenada
United Press International

WASHINGTON — All foreign troops, including some 250 members of the U.S. military, stationed on Grenada since the 1983 invasion will withdraw in September, the Reagan administration announced Thursday.

The withdrawal of the 250 U.S. troops and more than 400 troops from other Caribbean nations will begin in April "and be phased over a period of 5½ months," an announcement by the State Department said.

The United States, leading a force that included neighboring Caribbean countries, invaded Grenada Oct. 25, 1983, following the ouster and killing of leftist Prime Minister Maurice Bishop by more radical Marxist forces.

Aquino case renamed

MANILA, Philippines — Armed Forces Chief Gen. Fabian Ver, facing trial as an accessory to the murder of opposition leader Benigno Aquino, won a "psychological victory" Thursday by having his name dropped from the title of the case.

Justice Manuel Pamaran agreed with Ver's contention that using his name in the case title created the impression that the four-star general was charged as a principal rather than as an accessory.

Ver, 24 other soldiers and a civilian are charged in the Aug. 21, 1983, slayings of Aquino and Rolando Galman, the man prosecutors say the military tried to frame as Aquino's assassin.

Royal grip too tight

LONDON — Britain's Prince Philip is using a softer handshake because he's getting a sore wrist from pressing the flesh too often and too hard, a leading arthritis laboratory said Thursday.

The 63-year-old husband of Queen Elizabeth, who suffers from a kind of arthritis that inflames the joints, shakes hundreds of hands a week and has followed medical advice to greet well-wishers less robustly.

Philip visited the Strangeways Arthritis Laboratory at Cambridge Wednesday and was urged to abandon his usual hearty handshake in favor of a loose and less formal greeting.

Kim returning home

TOKYO (UPI) — South Korean opposition leader Kim Dae Jung, on the eve of his return home from exile, said Thursday he is ready to cooperate with President Chun Doo Hwan.

The opposition leader, looking tired after a long flight from the United States, told a crowded Tokyo news conference: "I strongly hope my return to Korea will not result in creating social chaos, but will result in stability."

Kim, his wife, Lee Hee Ho, and a 38-member delegation arrived in Tokyo Thursday for an overnight stop at an airport hotel.

COMING. THE NEW BOONE COUNTY BANK.

Soon you'll see a beautiful new addition in downtown Columbia when Boone County Bank expands its Main Bank building. The contemporary architecture of this 22,000 square foot enlargement melds with the old, unifying both buildings in a way symbolic of the Bank itself.

The spacious Bank lobby will house a new and innovative Financial Services area and Trust Department on the first floor, with Commercial, Consumer and Real Estate Loans on the upper floors — all designed to serve our customers' every financial need with convenience and quiet professionalism.

This major financial commitment to downtown Columbia expresses the Bank's confidence in the potential of our community.

Since 1857, a part of Columbia's past, and vitally interested in its present and its future.

Boone County Bank

PAGE DIMENSIONS

The page dummy forms in this workbook are drawn to scale to correspond with a six-column format approved by the American Newspaper Publishers Association as part of its Standard Advertising Unit program. The program is designed to convince newspaper publishers to adopt standard dimensions, which in turn makes it easier for national advertisers to place ads in newspapers. Columns are 12 picas, 2 points, and gutters are 1 pica (12 points). In the charts in this appendix, standard settings for such a page are listed. Numbers following decimal points are expressed in points, not tenths, so the base unit is 12, not 10. For example, 12.10 picas would not be the same as 13 picas. Instead, it would be 2 points narrower than 13 picas. Expressed another way, 12.10 picas plus 12.10 picas would equal 25.8.

GUTTER-TO-GUTTER COLUMN WIDTHS

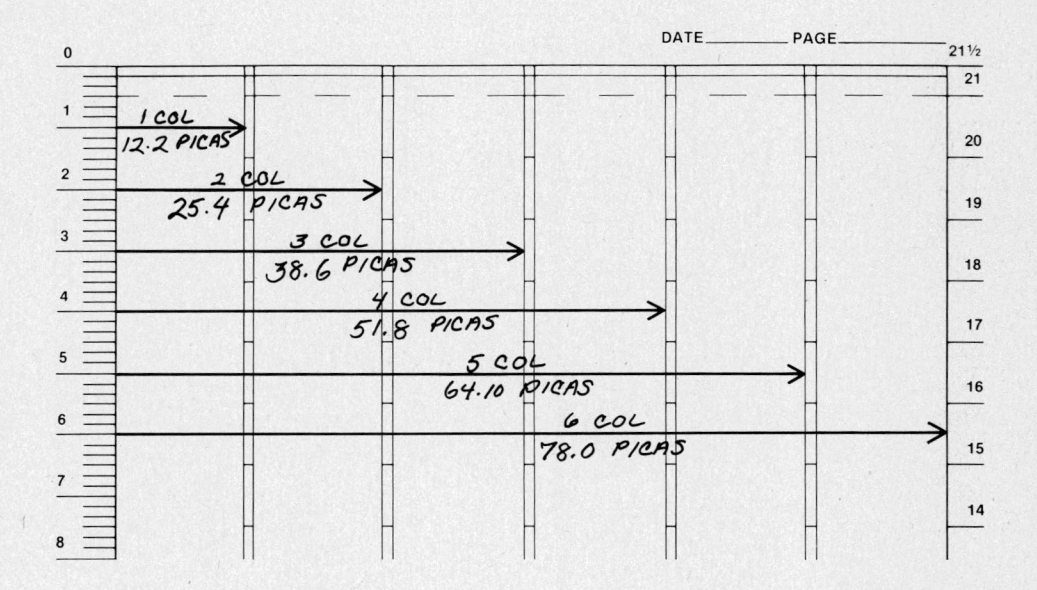

These measurements allow the editor to determine the exact width of pictures in picas and points. Thus, a three-column picture would be 38.6 picas wide. That allows the editor to calculate the exact depth of the picture in picas and points and provides the makeup artist with exact dimensions.

Understanding the gutter-to-gutter dimension system also allows the editor to make exact calculations for odd-measure settings of stories. Assuming that all gutters, even those between type wraps in boxed stories, are to remain at one pica, and assuming that one pica is needed on each side of the box to allow for the rule, such calculations are made simple. To eliminate the need to calculate the measure each time, these charts will serve as a handy reference guide:

ODD MEASURES (No Box)

Number of Type Wraps	Number of Columns	Setting
1	1	**12.2**
1	2	**25.4**
2	3	**18.9**
3	4	**16.7**
4	5	**15.5**
5	6	**14.10**

Note: Other combinations, such as three measures in five columns, are possible. That, however, would produce a setting of 21.1 picas, and anything in excess of 20 picas generally is considered too wide for easy legibility of newspaper text type.

ODD MEASURES (Boxed Stories)

Number of Type Wraps	Number of Columns	Setting
1	1	**10.2**
2	2	**11.2**
2	3	**17.10**
3	4	**15.11**
4	5	**14.11**
5	6	**14.5**

OTHER CALCULATIONS

The preceding charts are helpful in determining frequently used odd measures. The editor, however, has the option of making a picture any width, and in some cases that width will not conform to standard column widths. When that occurs, the editor must calculate the type setting of the story or stories to be placed beside the picture. Let's assume that the editor plans to run a picture 28 picas wide and place the story beside it in a five-column space. We know that five columns equals 65.3 picas. There must be a gutter of one pica between the picture and the story. Thus:

```
 64.10    (five columns)
-28.0     (picture width)
 36.10
 -1.0     (gutter)
 35.10    (space remaining for type)
```

We know that type should not be set 35.10 picas wide, so two wraps of type are necessary. That means another gutter will be needed:

```
 35.10
 -1.0     (second gutter)
 34.10    (space remaining for type)
÷ 2.0     (number of wraps of type)
 17.5     (type setting for story)
```

This would be the result:

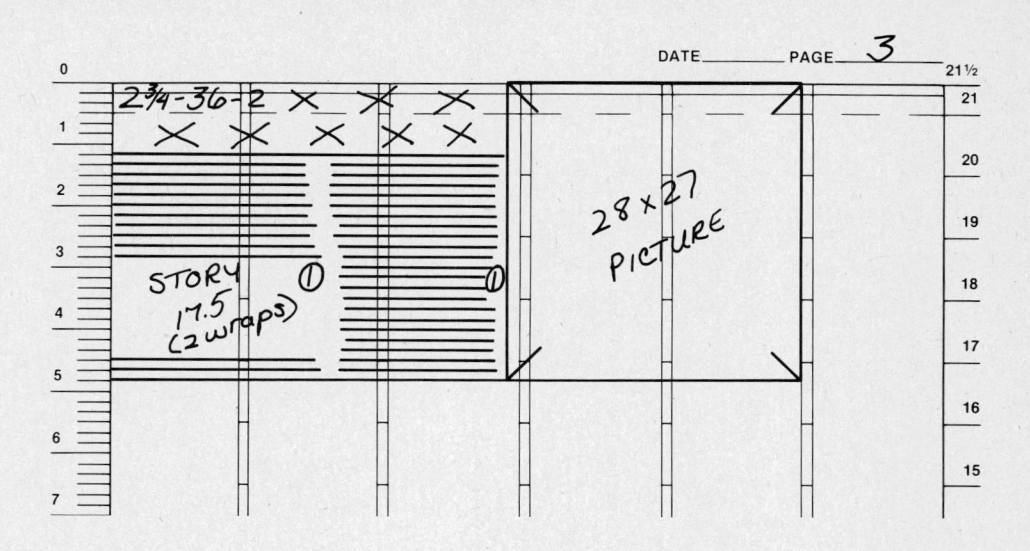

CUTLINE WIDTHS

Because outlines frequently are set larger than text type, and because they are brief, their width may exceed 20 picas. Here is a handy chart for determining cutline settings in our standard format:

Column Width	Number of Wraps	Setting
1	1	12.2
2	1	25.4
3	2	18.9
4	2	25.4
5	2	31.11
6	3	25.4

Cutline settings for boxed pictures or odd-measure pictures would have to be calculated using the system outlined earlier.

CALCULATING STORY LENGTHS

Editors with video display terminals have no trouble calculating story lengths; the computer does it for them. Editors who deal with typewritten copy must judge the length of a story before it is typeset. Typically, three typewritten lines of copy will produce about one column inch of type set 12.2 picas.

—301—

PN 4778 .B3 1986 wkbk.

DATE DUE			
JUN 15 '89			
AUG 10 '90			
SEP 09 2002			
OCT 10 2002			
SEP 25 2003			

PN 4778 .B3 1986 wkbk.